THE URBAN HOMESTEADING GUIDE TO HERBS

BUILDING YOUR OWN HERBAL APOTHECARY BY HERB GARDENING IN YOUR KITCHEN OR BACKYARD; GROW, HARVEST, STORE, AND CRAFT HERBAL ANTIBIOTICS AND ANTIVIRALS.

PUSHPA PUAR

SPECIAL BONUS!

Want This Bonus Book for Free?

Get <u>FREE</u> unlimited access to it and all of my new books by joining the Fan Base!

SCAN W/ YOUR CAMERA TO JOIN!

CONTENTS

Prologue   9
1. Introduction to Herbal Homesteading   17
2. Planning And Getting Things Ready   33
3. Part 1: Planting, Harvesting, and Storing   43
4. Part 11: Planting, Harvesting, and Storing   75
5. Pest Control, And Fertilizers   107
6. Herbal Recipes for Antibiotics And Antivirals   123
7. DIY Your Herbal Household Products   141
8. Making Money From Herbal Homesteading   153

Conclusion   161
References   163

PROLOGUE

"When the world wearies, and society fails to satisfy, there is always a garden."

— MINNIE AUMONIER

I believe human history has a lot to do with the places we live. There is something to be said for cultures' believing and relying on the power of nature to facilitate holistic healing.

The years I spent in my country of birth, India, as a small child, opened my eyes to the richness of nature. I grew up surrounded by forests, abundant in rich herbs and berries, and my senses attenuated the world around me in a different way. I saw, breathed, and lived in nature.

When I was ten, my family moved to Canada. On the journey to my new home, I remember worrying about being surrounded by busy streets and a different kind of lifestyle—one entirely disconnected from the larger environment which nourishes it. My worries were assuaged when I found a beautiful little farm awaiting us by our house.

My mother was born with a green thumb—something I can proudly say I have inherited. Over the next few decades, we grew herbs, spices, and condiments such as garlic, ginger, and cilantro on our farm. As a family, we manicured our home's lawn. Our policy was very simple. We believed in sustaining ourselves from the fruit of the earth. Dirt has never scared us—as a matter of fact, we look at it as one would an uncut diamond. If you nourish and preserve it, it will bless you in manifold ways.

My parents never imposed any limitations when it came to exploring and understanding soil. I grew up with the conscious understanding that soil was my home and my sustenance. I believed the very secret to life could be found atop tall trees, waiting to be uncovered upon climbing. I'd run around our farm, trailing my hands along the bark of tall pine trees to identify the sticky sap dripping down them. One day, I learned that they were nothing short of an antibiotic elixir.

I have always enjoyed spending time among flowers, plants, and trees. People have green thumbs, but I believe my very blood flows green. A little way down from where we lived, nature abounded in a secret, wild garden that was teeming with wild berries and the occasional scallion. We picked and ate them, treating each bite as a form of healing.

My mother and I loved to go for long walks down forgotten country roads, where she'd point out different herbs to me along the way. From Lizard's Tail to Elderberry, Mangler to Goat Weed, I only knew the world as a home to immensely mysterious life forms. In fact, I never stopped to think they'd have more uses than just looking "pretty."

The notion that these fragile things could carry so much healing within them was relatively unknown to me until one day, something happened. Calendula was one of my favorite flowers to grow in our garden. I could spend hours marveling at its cheerful yellow blooms. Then, one day. my mother told me that it also had many uses that exceeded its aesthetic pleasure. It felt as if I was a child on the verge of a momentous discovery.

I remember asking her, wide-eyed with curiosity, "What else does it do?"

She smiled and picked a petal. Turning to me, she said, "Sweetie, this is a ray floret. When you eat it, it works like a potion for your tummy."

Well, that sounded brilliant. I used to fall sick pretty often as a child. Every time I ate the merest thing outside the limits of home-cooked food, I'd wake up with terrible indigestion.

I scrunched up my features into a glorious scowl. How was I supposed to eat a flower? Was my mom pulling my leg? Before I could protest, she laughed. "Let's do a little magicking."

That night, she baked a fresh batch of banana muffins and tossed calendula petals into them. When I first bit into a hot muffin with its soft, fluffy texture, my eyes shot open, surprised. It tasted ever so slightly different. If I could literally describe how a hug might feel as "tangibly warm," I'd say that was the closest I got to it. From there, I learned to enjoy Calendula petals in homemade salads, muffins, and even a spot of tea now and then. A month after making it a part of my diet, my tummy was the strongest it had ever been.

Dear reader, it's been four decades since I began delving into the healing powers herbs have to offer. And, healing is not the only thing herbs can do. These little bunches of wonder can add flavor to your food, offer you nourishment, uplift your soul, *as well as heal you in the most wholesome ways possible*. Homesteading and growing my own herbs have become my way of life. After reading about the wonder of herbs and their intrinsic value, I hope you will feel the same way.

I have a dear friend who faced the annoyance of a persistent eating disorder. When this disorder culminated in a severe case of acid reflux, she went the conventional route. Unfortunately, the medications she was prescribed made the immediate reflux go away—which made her feel that every time she faced acid reflux, she could just take medicine. In a very dangerous way, this validated her eating disorder without addressing it.

My primary goal in writing this book is to help people such as my friend, you, and others to achieve freedom from the outward and latent side effects of the modern pills and packets that come with short-term healing. What you will learn has helped me overcome my own struggles with health and has equipped me to take better care of those who are dear to me.

I know things always seem overwhelming at the onset. If you have found your way to this book, there is a chance you already know the benefits of herbal medicine. You might want to take a step into herbal homesteading, but cannot do so without a sound knowledge of what herbs are, how you can identify them, or which diseases they cure.

You might be considering turning your outdoor space into a prolific herbal garden, but without the basics of planting and nurturing information, you feel as if you don't know where to begin. You may have heard about these wonderful tinctures and ointments that carry the healing properties of herbs within them. This has made you eager to prepare your own, if only you could find out how!

For all these reasons and more, I am here to guide you, as you delve into the whimsical world of herbology. The strategies we will discuss in this book will help you immensely and give you the confidence you need to begin your homesteading journey.

Our journey together will prepare you, by introducing you to herbal homesteading along with the means to identify herbs and their benefits. We will cover which herbs you can plant, depending on your regional climatic zones, how to nurture them, and how you can harvest and store them for future purposes. To top it off, we will also "take a gander" at soothing recipes for herbal remedies and the methods whereby you can make your own herbal cleaners and body care products.

There are three sections to this book. The first introduces you to herbal homesteading and explains how to plan and prepare your garden for the season ahead. In the second, we'll talk about how to grow herbs and how to store them. We'll also cover pest and disease management, fertilizing the garden, and composting. Herbal treatments, cleaning products, and skin care items created at home are all covered in the book's third and final section, which also includes information about how to generate money via herbal homesteading.

Before we dive in, let me quickly run over each chapter we will cover together.

Chapter One will give you a complete and detailed overview of how herbal homesteading works, and what it entails. You will find that many of us unnecessarily complicate the idea of "homesteading" from a very furnished perspective. Yet, when it comes to survival, we humans have surprisingly basic needs. This chapter will be the cornerstone to increasing your confidence in homesteading.

Chapter Two will be all about the financials. Budgetary constraints are legitimate, but growing herbs need not cost you immense amounts of time, land, money, and other resources. Some herbs are surprisingly resilient and will grow in many different conditions, as long as you give them some tender loving care. Our goal for this chapter is to ensure that your homesteading garden is one that fits comfortably within your budget.

In **Chapter Three**, we will begin our ascent into the different forms of planting, harvesting, and storing herbs. We will talk about twenty herbs. In continuation, **Chapter Four** will cover twenty additional herbs you can grow, care for, and harvest.

Chapter Five is going to open your eyes to the different issues which plants face, particularly during their developmental phase. You will learn about pest control, the use of fertilizers, and methods to keep insects at bay.

Herbal recipes, with a focus on herbal antibiotics and antivirals, will be the stars of **Chapter Six**. In **Chapter Seven**, we will move on to the art of DIY, a fun chapter on how you can make your own cleaners, house supplies, and body care products using herbs. Finally, in **Chapter Eight**, you will learn that there is even more to homesteading. Profit generation is a very real advantage and can become a side hustle, or even the main way of life for you.

The Urban Homesteading Guide to Herbs is here to dispel all your homesteading worries, one by one. What you need to do is keep reading from the perspective of "I can do this, because now, I will have the knowledge I need to homestead." The biggest changes happen with the tiniest steps, so be excited! Your adventure begins at the turn of the page.

Come. Let us begin.

INTRODUCTION TO HERBAL HOMESTEADING

"The healing comes from nature and not from the physician. Therefore, the physician must start from nature with an open mind."

— PARACELSUS

At the very onset of my herbal homesteading journey, there was one question that I was asked repeatedly. People were naturally curious to know why I wanted to grow my own herbs. When I told them I was interested in delving into their medicinal properties, they were nothing short of amazed. Their unanimous reactions were always along the lines of, "But why do you need voodoo healing when you have access to proper medicine?" It has taken a lot of time to dispel this utterly wrong conception associated with the forms of healing that turn to nature. If anything, *all medicine comes from the world around us*. Some of us, including me, choose to go "as close to nature as it gets", and for specific reasons.

WHY CHOOSE HERBS OVER MODERN MEDICINES?

Natural medicine marries nature's nourishing and non-invasive tools of therapy to heal not just the apparent symptoms of a disease but also the **underlying conditions**. On the other hand, orthodox medicine continues to be tied to the mainstream model, wherein healthcare professionals are only concerned with treating people based on the patient's immediate symptoms.

The side effects of traditional remedies are well known; however, most people are unaware of the possible negative effects of the drugs they are taking. The lack of transparent information from the conventional healthcare system may well be responsible for this. Medicine information sheets may be all the patient has to go on, when it comes to learning about their medication. Since dangerous chemicals are not used in the production of natural medicine, these remedies do not put your body out of balance.

As I cited in the example of my tummy ache, from the book's prologue, it is unusual for orthodox medicine to consider the underlying issues behind a specific ailment. If you have a stomach ache, you get medicine for the stomach ache. It could be that the cause of this stomach ache is something entirely unrelated to the immediate pain you are experiencing.

Natural medicine will go beyond your immediate issue, to look at your entire system. Perhaps it is psychosomatic, or has occurred due to an imbalance in another organ. When you consider wellness, you must look at the entire being instead of just the component parts. Natural medicine has built itself around the philosophy of entirety, which is part of why it is so effective.

Most of the components included in herbal remedies are ones that your body produces regularly. Your body's physiological process is strengthened, and your immune system is bolstered when you use natural medications. A well-functioning immune system means that your body is strong enough to protect itself against diseases and illnesses.

Natural medicines have been around for centuries longer than conventional allopathic cures. If their effectiveness was only the subject of ridicule or "voodoo," then they would have become redundant much earlier. On the contrary, however, they have been in use for over ten thousand years.

All throughout its long existence, the healing power of natural medicine has been credited for how non-invasive it is. Natural medicine does not require the human body to be invaded by needles and foreign objects to relieve symptoms. Neither is it concerned with flooding the body with chemical components. It only uses what is sourced from nature and is entirely reliant on ingredients that are in their most intrinsically wholesome form. A related component known as remedial massaging works in tandem with natural medicine, to relieve acute and chronic pain from different body parts, enhance body functions, and stimulate overall healing.

Orthodox medicine can often act in clandestine ways to suppress symptoms of an illness. Instead of treating the root cause of an issue, it simply clamps down on the apparent indications. The problem is—even though your symptoms are suppressed, the illness still persists below the surface. If the medicine you're taking doesn't work, your symptoms may return or even become worse. As a result, you'll find yourself in a never-ending loop of trying various drugs in an attempt to relieve your initial symptoms.

It helps to remember that these new drugs may have additional detrimental consequences of their own. You could take immediate relief and be satisfied, but the symptoms are not going to be suppressed forever. They *will* return—so it is always better for you to look at what is causing the symptoms in the first place. The answer to this question lies in natural medicine. Identifying and addressing the pathophys-iology of your ailment is a natural medicine tenet.

In India, the country I come from, an entire branch of medi-cine is dedicated to curing ailments with herbs. *Ayurveda*, the Sanskrit term for herbal remedies, refers to *ayur* (life) and *veda* (knowledge). It means knowledge of life. Put simply, this means restoring the natural balance of life through the gifts of nature. It is only natural that we, as children of nature, should turn to her, looking for cures for our afflictions.

Ancient doctors and surgeons were avid watchers of nature. They saw how animals and beasts sought out leaves and bark to heal their wounds and cure their diseases. The medicine-men observed how the indigenous people sought out specific roots, herbs and flowers, extracted their juices and applied them to sores and wounds as poultices. Nature was their teacher, and she did not deprive them. The vast repertoire of natural remedies is inexhaustive and still under research.

The rain-washed, cloud-covered, blue mountains of the Western Ghats and the extensive valleys of the snowclad Himalayas, in India, abound with a treasure trove of natural remedies. Herbs, roots, flowers, berries, and seeds, all harvested and developed into various remedies, are used to detoxify our systems, purify the blood, and rejuvenate our bodies and minds. The whole tenet of the science of Ayurveda, or the natural remedy of which yoga is an integral part, is centered on the concept that disease is a stressful condition, an imbalance of the natural state, and we should use natural products to restore it back to its healthful vigorous state.

This is where homesteading steps in. By homesteading, you bring a little of the earth closer to your home. By getting closer to the soil, you embrace a more fulfilling and productive life.

What Homesteading Entails?

In April 2022, the British Prime Minister, Boris Johnson visited India. While he was there, he went to the Sabarmati Ashram, the hermitage of Mahatma Gandhi. Gandhi is widely known as a champion of peace and for spearheading India's freedom from British rule in India. But, more than this, his philosophy of self-reliance, of shunning industrialization and reverting back to nature to reinstitute our traditional way of living has become more and more relevant today. He did not have faith in things that were mass-produced and believed that intense industrialization would deplete natural resources more quickly, thereby creating hardship and inevitable chains of command. When Prime Minister Johnson spun threads on the *Charkha* (spinning wheel), a symbol of self-reliance promoted by Gandhi, he displayed that the harmonized way of living—where we function as an integral component of nature and our surroundings—is increasingly endorsed by people worldwide.

Homesteading, in principle, upholds self-reliance. One may grow one's food, generate one's electricity, harvest rainwater for household purposes, raise livestock or build one's home from the resources available in one's surroundings. Homesteaders encourage their families to live a community-friendly life and to have a better understanding of the environment around them.

People homestead for different reasons. Some love to grow their own vegetables and herbs, and some do it for extra food on the table. However, they all share a common bond with nature and things natural.

The packaged food we eat, the milk our babies drink, and the medicines we take are loaded with chemicals, artificial colors, and stabilizers. They have to be to increase their shelf-life and to produce things for the masses. But foods lose their natural appeal and nutritional values, and who doesn't know that all chemical medicines have side effects, in the long run, some of which are debilitating?

We do not even need to cook our food anymore, nor do we have to visit stores and groceries to buy them. Everything can be ordered online, and delivered to us in the comfort of our homes. Gradually, we are becoming more sedentary, and dependent on using gadgets for almost everything, from running television channels to driving cars. One fine morning we may discover that the only use for our hands is to tap keyboards and the handheld remotes of electronic gadgets. It's unsettling, right?

I go to upmarket grocery stores that stock "organic" food and herbs, because I don't want my food and the food I serve my family to be laden with insecticides and harmful chemicals. There in these stores, the same vegetables and roots that grow abundantly along the ponds and lakes, and the same herbs that flourish so easily in the backyard are sold at twice the price of "normal" products. Those of you who have had a similar experience know how annoying this can be.

No doubt, people like us get frustrated by the current way of life. I tell my children about the food we ate when my family ate when I was young, describing in detail their tastes, flavors, colors, and juiciness. My mother raised hens and ducks, because she wanted to give us fresh eggs for breakfast. We had cows and horses on our farm, and I milked the cows and rode my horse to the market.

We cannot all live on farms and villages, but espousing a more rooted way of living is not absolutely impossible in cities and towns. Homesteading is not about having a lot of space to grow your things or to raise a few hens. It is more about adopting a lifestyle. You do some magic with your hands and relish the fruits of your endeavor and it soon turns into a passion.

So, people homestead. Whether they are disillusioned by the artificiality of contemporary living or are in search of a deeper connection with roots, they all learn the old-fashioned way of living close to the earth and enjoy doing it.

The feeling of soft crumbling earth on your fingers, the smell of the first rains, and the joy of watching the first crops are all deeply satisfying and gratifying beyond measure. As one gets closer to the earth, one cannot escape its embrace again.

When my friend, Arni, chose to live simply, in the University town of Berkeley, his parents and friends thought his ideas were preposterous and fanciful. Arni started off by living in a tent. Then, he built his house; it was open and airy, allowing the sunshine in and reducing his dependence on electricity.

He generated his own electricity by using a hand-operated motor and harvested rainwater for household use. Arni leased a bit of land, where he grew herbs and crops. It was of some significance when he said research is akin to cultivating the land—the most promising resource we have. Perhaps he knew; he was a professor of physics at Berkeley University.

Over the years, Arni's friends and some of his colleagues discovered the joy of living a similar life, and they formed a community. They grew herbs and plants such as citrus, ginger, thyme, primrose, curcumin, and dandelion. They were aware of the medicinal properties of these herbs, and before long, they were preparing capsules in collaboration with a pharmaceutical company.

Then came the pandemic. Suddenly, all around, people were falling sick and dying in their hundreds. The new virus proliferated unbridled in the environment, unrecognized and unchecked by the human immune system.

When orthodox medicine failed to provide a cure for the viral onslaught, people tried improving and boosting their immunity through traditional herbal medicines. Expert immunologists talked about the immune-boosting capabilities of certain herbs such as ginger, dandelion, and citrus. Even a frangible flower, such as the dandelion was found to block the SARS-CoV2 virus from entering a human cell, as was shown in various research.

Can I Grow Herbs, Too?

You may be a student, renting a shared apartment in the city, or a retired person with a lot of free time on your hands. However, if you enjoy the greenery and want to have a little splash of color on your windowsill, or a fully-fledged herb garden in the backyard, you are certainly the person to start an herbal homestead. The desire to soothe the eyes, titillate the taste buds, and pique the senses with the freshness of aromatic herbs are all enough reasons to encourage someone who wants to start an herbal homestead of their own.

Like any other endeavor, the idea of herbal homesteading may fill your mind with doubts and questions. Concepts such as, it is difficult to grow herbs, and they need a lot of care, time, and patience may plague us. Let me assure you that growing herbs, once learned correctly, is easy and requires less time and effort than many other tasks. Most of the time, they manage on their own and are no bother at all.

Myths to Bust

- Herbal homesteading needs a lot of space.
- Bright sunshine is a prerequisite for growing herbs.
- I need garden soil for homesteading.
- I need plastic containers.
- I need many containers to grow the herbs that I want.
- I have to water them daily.
- They die easily.
- Harvesting them is highly technical.

Facts to get Started

Herbal homesteading does not require a lot of space. Grow your herbs on your windowsill. If your windows do not have ledges, install a window box or more easily attach a planter's box to the window. Parsley, thyme, varieties of basil, and strawberries are some plants that grow well in windowsill boxes.

Grow herbs on the patio, on your balcony, or even indoors in your kitchen, near the kitchen window. Plenty of herbs, such as chives, parsley, and garden cress, grow indoors. Having a kitchen garden right in your kitchen is a marvelous idea of herbal homesteading.

Most herbs need seven to eight hours of sunshine to produce essential oils. However, herbs such as basil, cilantro, and parsley need shade, particularly in the hot summer afternoons. Keeping your indoor plants near a window that allows maximum sunshine to fall on them for at least the biggest portion of the day would be the correct choice. Otherwise, get yourself a "grow light" that optimizes sunshine and ensures the growth of your herbs.

What soil is the best to grow the herbs? Aromatic herbs need well-drained soil, and your garden soil may not be well-drained. This could make the roots moldy. So, rather than using garden soil, use well-drained organic potting mixes that are scientifically prepared; they are readily available in plant nurseries or online.

But how will I pot them? Most people use almost anything to grow their greens in, and the choices can be as varied as used soft drink bottles or mineral water bottles cut in half, plastic containers, metal cans, and wooden crates. Although herbs can grow in all of these containers, the best choice is a terracotta pot with drainage holes.

There is no need to have many containers to grow different herbs. Although it is true that some species require special potting, most will grow together perfectly well in the same container.

The other concern is watering the herbs. Surprisingly, herbs do not need much water, and overwatering will surely kill them. The trick is to insert your finger into the soil, once every day, to check if it's moist. If the soil feels dry and loose, water them thoroughly. If the soil feels moist skip watering the plants. Regular but superficial watering will make the roots weak. They tend to come up to the soil's surface instead of forming a deep underground network of strong root systems.

One may buy saplings or seedlings to grow in the first few batches. Upon gaining some experience with gardening, one may shift to seeds to have stronger, more vigorous plants. Herbs can be annual, biennial, and perennial. The annual varieties, such as basil and rosemary, complete their life cycles in one year. The biennial varieties, such as parsley and chives, live for two years, and the perennial varieties, such as mint, oregano, and thyme, live for many years. Carefully choosing your herbs will ensure your kitchen garden never falls short of fresh herbs. A container full of fresh green herbs with a fragrant aromatic flavor is a planter's delight to watch growing.

Don't be afraid to harvest your herbs; it requires no great skill. Just nip off the top of the herbs cleanly; this allows the dormant leaf buds to grow. For annual varieties, clip the stems regularly but prune your perennials well during the warm months.

Gardening is one of those works that you learn in the field. Plants are patient teachers, tenacious and strong. They do not give up easily and can withstand hardship and oversight.

When you work with them, you learn their traits, the conditions they love, and the practices that encourage strong roots and lavish foliage.

Herbal homesteading need not be limited to growing kitchen herbs. Indeed, it can be the beginning of a whole new journey for you. If you discover your passion for growing herbs and educate yourself about their beneficial uses, you can also take up herbalism as your vocation.

An herbalist is a self-employed individual who specializes in growing herbs and knowing their medicinal values. They train themselves in the art of "wildcrafting" or plucking the right varieties of herbs from the wild. Herbs are used for a variety of purposes, from enhancing the flavor of food and drink to making medicines and cosmetics. They are also widely used in the gastronomic, pharmaceutical, and cosmetics industries. The nutraceutical industry uses herbs to produce food supplements, functional foods, medicinal foods, and farmaceuticals. These products are marketed in syrups, tablets, and capsules as antioxidants to prevent malignancies, improve immunity, and foster general well-being. Your expertise may find its use in any of these sectors.

Study and research herbs. Take up a career as a teaching professional of herbal remedies. Chiropractic, naturopathy, and nutritional counselling could be other career options for you. There is a branch of science called "ethnobotany". It is a subgenre of anthropology, a specialized knowledge of how plants are used in different cultures worldwide. They study the history of indigenous plants in different cultures and how people used plants and medicinal herbs to maintain and restore health as well as to cure different ailments.

We all know how forests are cut down, and rivers are made to change their course to satisfy the greed of power-hungry consumers. We are constantly losing biosphere reserves, and depleting the planet of the vital resources that have nurtured different species, ourselves included, for thousands of years. Any step, however small it might be, to revert this large-scale destruction will help to restore the health of our planet. We are all an integral part of our planetary system, and our knowledge of its natural resources will help to preserve the different biological communities.

If I am talking about big things and self-sufficiency, remember our humble beginning—a container full of fresh herbs adorning our windowsill.

2

PLANNING AND GETTING THINGS READY

All enterprises start with planning and organization. Herbal homesteading is no exception to this. There can be so many considerations—which herbs will be suitable for your environment, how you are going to plan, what things will you need to buy, which season to choose for planting, and most of all, do you have the budget necessary to start your project.

Let us devote some time to discussing all of these vital issues and to finding out how we can progress in our attempt at farming, however small-scale that may be.

SELECTION OF SPACE FOR HOMESTEAD

In his last posting, my father-in-law stayed at a sprawling bungalow in Ellicott City, Baltimore. It came with a whopping ten-acre garden of fruit trees, vines, and creepers. My in-laws were avid planters, and they used this space fully, to grow herbs, marrows, and exotic veggies and fruits. Post-retirement, they shifted to an apartment in New York. Although big, it was an apartment after all, with relatively circumscribed space for gardening.

My mother-in-law could not bring many of her exotic collections with her, but it did not deter her from growing a beautiful urban homestead. They had herbs and plants everywhere—on the walls, the kitchen top, windowsills, the verandah, and in their tiny backyard.

They never lacked in indulging their guests and family with innovative epicurean delights that they sourced right from their garden. It was fun to watch them brew something on the stove, scuttle to one of the innumerable pots and containers, pluck a few sprigs of rosemary, chives, or thyme, sniff them, and then toss them into the cooking pot.

Since the cessation of formal homesteading in the US, in 1976, large-scale homesteading has become a limited concept for the current generation. There is just not enough land for an average individual, and total self-sufficiency may be a distant dream. This means that you may be unable to satisfy all of your requirements with whatever free space is available to you for homesteading. Even so, you *can* manage to reduce your dependence on external sources of nourishment by growing your own things.

Perhaps your backyard is half an acre, and you need some space for your children to play and for you to host an occasional barbecue. You can still fully use the rest of the space to grow your herb garden.

Grow citrus, peppermint, chamomile, calendula, plantain, and strawberries to adorn your garden, and you'll earn accolades from your friends and family alike. You can keep a few chickens; your children will learn to take care of birds and small animals, and you can also enjoy fresh eggs for breakfast.

For children, it's exciting to collect fresh farm produce in small wicker baskets. You can teach them gardening skills that they will cherish. On the whole, you can have an exciting time with your family and get some fresh farm produce as a bonus.

It is always a good idea to begin small. It is possible to grow a salsa garden, replete with tomatoes, dill, and bell peppers, on your balcony!

As you progress, you can evaluate your work from time to time and make small changes or additions. You gain experience and learn to do things better, grander, and faster.

Budgeting Your Urban Homestead

I have a terrible habit of buying many things before starting a new project, and I often do it on impulse. For instance, I once decided to embroider dresses. I knew nothing about sewing, let alone embroidery, but that did not dampen my enthusiasm. I went out and bought the most expensive sewing kit and fabrics without thoroughly researching what I needed. Needless to say, I got nowhere with my knitting project and wasted my money.

I have since learned to dedicate a little time to careful fact-finding before an endeavor, and budgeting is one of its essential features.

You may already have an idea of what you want to get out of your venture as an urban homesteader. If you do not, I advise you to give it some thought. Homesteading, especially urban homesteading, needs careful consideration and planning. Having a few pots of herbs can be a very different concept from running a fully-fledged greenhouse.

Some of us would like to raise a few chickens; some may want to install solar panels to generate electricity for self-consumption, and yet others may be excited about beekeeping. Your budget plans will vary in each of these circumstances.

For a simple herbal garden, all you need to invest in are a few containers, soil, compost, insecticides and pesticides, as well as saplings or seeds. Herbs do not need much water or care. The return is high compared to investment.

After you decide what kind of herbal homestead you want, the next step is to budget for it.

How do I budget for my mini urban farm?

You cannot compromise on the quality of the soil or seeds. Most of us want to grow our own greens, because we want to avoid chemical fertilizers, pesticides, or GM crops. So, selecting good quality, non-GM seeds is a priority.

The worst setback for a farm can be dying crops, so know that good crops need good soil conditions. Oftentimes, crops can die due to a deficiency of nutrients in the soil. For heavy feeders such as tomatoes, it's essential to replenish the nutrients in the soil.

The trick is to generate compost from vegetable and fruit peels, coffee grounds, egg shells, newspaper, cardboard, paper, straw, and pieces of untreated wood. If you raise chickens, you can even use their droppings. In time, you can prepare your own potting soil.

To save more from your annual harvest, you can propagate herbs from their stems or seeds during spring, reducing the cost of buying fresh plants. Herbs flower in autumn, and their leaves become smaller and more bitter. This is the time they go to seed. Collect and save the seeds for the next season; you can even swap them with your friends for some new varieties. An online search will enable you to find a venue for suitable seed swaps. You can also sell some of the rooted cuttings and start earning money from your herbal garden.

Any step you take will be a step forward. Learn to preserve fruits, berries, and herbs by making jams, jellies, wines, and pickles.

Harvesting rainwater and using refurbished household containers for potting will be cost-effective for a beginner. While this lowers the basic outlay, you may still want to buy implements such as a wheelbarrow, sprayers, rakes, etc. Do not shy away from borrowing implements from your neighbors, at least initially—sometimes in exchange for your farm produce.

Remember the basic tenet of homesteading: encourage simple living and a community feeling. You grow your food and share it with your friends, family, and neighbors. This is an opportunity for you to build an interdependent, solid community.

Think about how else you can cut back on expenditures. Gardening is an excellent exercise. If you spend considerable time gardening, you may give up a gym membership.

Encouraging a simple lifestyle and returning to your roots summons the joy of rediscovering yourself. It differs from the glitzy and fast way of life to which we are otherwise accustomed. When we settle into it, we consciously opt for a healthier lifestyle. We realize that the latest mobiles, gadgets, and expensive clothes are draining our hard-earned money, and are otherwise valueless. Spend cautiously on these items to save your budget.

Plan Your Garden

Many herbs, such as basil, mint, curry leaves and fennel, serve a dual purpose for culinary and medicinal needs; they are flavor enhancers when added to dishes and improve digestive functions. Basil and calendula have excellent medicinal properties and are very pleasing to look at. When you begin with an herbal homestead, these are some of the best ones to start. They are hardy, easy to grow, and low on maintenance.

Start with one or two herbs annually and, once you gain experience, challenge yourself to try newer and more exotic varieties. Plants are like children; you learn as you raise them.

Investing in ready-made plants is easier than growing them from seeds. Do a little research on which plant nursery has the best reputation in your location. Enquire if they avoid genetically modified or hybrid seeds. Visit the nurseries, study the plants, and decide on the ones that grab your attention.

Before you buy a plant, find out if it suits your home environment and weather. The "cultural requirements" of herbs are the conditions they need to survive and thrive. Some medicinal herbs need six to seven hours of sunlight, whereas others can grow in the shade. They thrive in different soil, and water requirements vary.

Plants can still tolerate a little deviation from optimal soil and water requirements, but drastic weather conditions will kill them. Tropical herbs will die in colder climates, and herbs that thrive in colder weather conditions will not survive in hot weather.

Each climatic zone has its own set of herbs. Before buying them, look into the specificities of which zone your herb belongs. You will find a wide range of varieties within your geographic location, so choose herbs that are well-adjusted to the local climate. For example, if you live in Maryland, perennials such as fennel, thyme, oregano, sage, and tarragon can withstand the local winters well, but not holy basil, kafir lime, mint, or lemongrass.

Would you like to start practicing as an herbalist, making and selling your medicines to others? In an urban setting with a compact space, you have to decide the number of drugs you need to make, which herbs you need, and how much space you will need. For instance, a patch of two by eight feet yard is enough to produce a few good harvests of spearmint for around ten people (How To Plan And Plant A Medicinal Garden, 2019).

The easiest perennials, to begin with, are rosemary, mint, chives, and oregano. Annuals such as basil, coriander, and parsley are bountiful, therapeutic, and savory. They thrive in warmer conditions. Sowing annual varieties every three weeks will ensure a steady supply of crops throughout the summer season.

Annual plants flower when watered or exposed to sunlight. Most herbs are Mediterranean and hence do not need much water. Check for moisture every day or two. Do not let the soil get completely dry; rehydration is difficult.

Flowers attract bees to pollinate them and produce seeds. Thyme, catnip, lavender, hyssop, and rosemary flowers are some of the flowers that are popular with bees. Some herbs, such as mint, block the growth of other plants and need their own pot.

Besides the seeds or saplings, you will need to buy pots or containers with drainage holes. Drill a hole at the bottom if there is not one. You do not need to cover the hole with shards or gravel, before adding the soil mix. This can block proper drainage. Simply, lay a paper towel or newspaper over the hole to stop the soil from getting washed away, and then add thoroughly moistened soil mix and plant the seeds. Enhance your soil further with a layer of mulch an inch from the stems to retain moisture.

Terracotta pots are the best, but you can also use recyclable materials such as Styrofoam cups, coffee cups, and yogurt tubs as "seed-starter" containers. Polyurethane foam containers are cheap and crack-resistant and these pots insulate the root system from extremes of temperature.

A large and deep container can hold many types of herbs. Get adventurous and combine "thrillers, spillers, and fillers" in a single container.

A *thriller* is a statement plant of shape and color, such as geraniums. They grace the centerpiece of a large container. *Fillers,* such as parsley, peppers, or licorice fill up the space. The *spillers* at the edge of the container spill over, giving an opulent and luxurious look. Gorgeous spillers such as sweet potatoes and zinnias give a colorful, full-blown, and perfect look pouring over the edge of the container. A few of these containers will embellish the home, soothing your eyesight and attending to your culinary and medicinal needs.

Go creative with combinations, paying attention to their need for sun and shade. Flowering herbs need bright sunlight, but colorful leafy plants favor shade. The best combinations are herbs with luxurious leaves and long blooming perennial flowers, such as lavender for timeless beauty. Plant five to six plants in an 18–24" container.

Besides a medicinal garden, plan for a salsa, salad, or pizza garden. A salad garden, for instance, grows tomatoes, chives, dill, and coriander. How about an edible flower garden with nasturtiums, rose, saffron, or marigold?

Diluted fish emulsion, compost tea, and seaweed extract are all suitable fertilizers. Spray the leaves with twice-diluted preparations of these solutions.

3

PART 1: PLANTING, HARVESTING, AND STORING

I n this chapter, we will discuss planting, harvesting, and storing some of the more common herbs.

BEGINNER'S PARADISE

Basil, ginger, comfrey, oregano, and many other herbs are remarkable for their healing properties. Ginger enhances the flavor of food and helps to reduce coughs, aches, pains, and sore throat. Comfrey, on the other hand, is a hardy perennial with medicinal values. These herbs are easy for starting any homesteading adventure.

Basil

Basil, one of the oldest and most noble herbs, is rich in essential oils, such as cinnamate, citronellol, geraniol, etc. In

India, it is offered to deities and is considered holy. Many ayurvedic medicines use basil for its medicinal value. Italian, Mediterranean and Thai cuisines also use basil during food preparation to enhance flavor and nutritional value.

Benefits of Basil

- Basil leaves mixed with sandalwood paste and rose water and placed on the face is a curative for acne and pimples, due to the antibacterial, anti-inflammatory, and cleansing properties of the leaves.
- It is rich in flavonoid antioxidants that check cell aging and DNA damage in the cells, and it strengthens the immune system. Basil leaves are used to treat coughs and colds.
- Also due to its anti-inflammatory properties, basil leaves protect against heart diseases, joint inflammation, and inflammatory bowel diseases.
- It aids in food digestion.

Planting Basil

There are wide varieties of basil, including sweet basil, lemon basil, Italian basil, holy basil, and Thai basil, etc. All are rich in medicinal properties. Typically, it is grown in the US as a kitchen herb, both in and outdoors. This annual plant grows quickly and its seed-to-harvest time is usually three to four weeks.

- Sow a few seeds in the center of a seed starter pot, four to eight weeks before the date of the last frost. Use ¼" of dry seed starter mix.
- Water to keep the seeds moist until they germinate.
- A plastic starting container with a fitted lid retains humidity and temperature, facilitating germination. About 70°F of ambient temperature is suitable for seed germination.
- Once seedlings appear, remove the plastic lid of the pot and expose the seedlings to sunlight. Keep the soil moist with periodic spraying. Wait for the true leaves to appear.
- After the leaves come out, pot your best plants in your container.
- Choose a container where you can plant the saplings 12–16" apart, to allow enough sunlight and air for each of them, or bed them.
- Plant basil with other herbs, such as tomatoes, oregano, lettuce, or peppers to get the best products of both.
- Enrich ordinary garden soil with compost to make a well-drained potting mixture. Moisten the soil.
- Dig about a 6" hole so the roots can take hold of the soil and support the plants. With your hands, press the soil gently to secure the plants in place.

Caring for basil

Sunlight, 70°F of temperature, and frequent watering are essential to care for basil. Place them in shade in the scorching heat.

Water thoroughly at least once per week, and more frequently for containers. Water all your herbs early in the morning. One to two inches of mulch preserves moisture and adds to the pot's beauty.

Basil does not need fertilizers. A light fertilizer once a month for the container and twice a season for the beds is sufficient for basil.

Harvesting

Pinch the leaves from the tip after the appearance of two true leaves. Trimming helps in the luxurious growth of basil.

"Bolting" refers to when a crop prematurely grows flower stalks and produces seeds. Pinch off the flowers 1" below the stem. Once the flowers appear, the leaves tend to become smaller and bitter. Bolting can be checked by watering the plants adequately and keeping them in the shade during the hottest part of the day.

Harvest regularly, check the flowers, and maintain the shape of the shrub.

Storing

Basil is annual, though you should chop and freeze it with olive oil for winter. The leaves will retain moisture and flavor when frozen.

Ginger

Ginger, a rhizome, is full of flavor and medicinal properties. Some use its root in savory dishes, such as marinated fish as well as in meat preparations, salad dressings, soups, stir fry, and pickles. Sweet dishes are not exempt from the richness of ginger's flavor—smoothies, cakes, biscuits, and alcohol mixes all use ginger to enhance their flavor and taste. Ginger-infused tea is also a household remedy for coughs and colds.

Benefits

- Ginger settles an upset stomach. It is used to ease pregnancy, post-surgery, and chemotherapy nausea and vomiting.
- Its anti-inflammatory properties check joint pains. Topical ginger preparations rather than oral preparations are used for this purpose.
- Ginger tea and extracts in medicine are remedies for coughs, colds, and flu symptoms.
- It relieves menstrual cramps.
- It soothes skin burns.
- It lowers blood sugar in Type 2 diabetes.

- It contains essential minerals and vitamins, such as B3, B6, Niacin, Riboflavin, folates, Vitamin C, potassium, phosphorus, magnesium, and Zinc.
- Ginger is eaten raw, dried, and ground to make powders as in spices, tablets, and capsules, and its liquid is extracted to make syrups.

Planting Ginger

Ginger loves well-drained and moist soil that is rich in organic matter and warm, humid climates. It needs 2–5 hours of sunlight daily. Early spring is the best time to grow ginger.

To sow ginger, take a piece of healthy, fleshy, organic ginger. Soak it overnight in warm water and cut it into smaller pieces, taking care that each piece has a bud. Plant them 8" apart and 2– 4" deep in potting mix, with their eyes facing upward.

When shoots appear, transplant them, along with the soil, into your garden bed. Choose a location that enjoys direct sunlight and warmth.

Water the plants periodically and thoroughly, but do not water them daily since overwatering can rot young roots. A light liquid fertilizer once every two weeks will suffice for optimal plant growth.

If you want to pot your ginger plants, choose a deep container with about a 10-gallon capacity—plant the rhizomes ¾" deep in the soil. Cover the pot with a cling wrap to retain moisture, particularly if you live in a dry climate. Remove the cling film once new shoots start appearing. Alternatively, use mulch.

Harvesting

Once the plant is about 3' in height, your ginger is ready for harvesting. It will be mild in taste. For anything stronger, wait until the plant is mature. It usually takes about eight to ten weeks in optimal conditions.

To harvest, dig around the rhizome and cut the more mature sections off it, leaving the younger roots and shoots undamaged. Ginger is allowed to mature until the second growing season when the roots can be fully harvested.

Storing

- Store ginger in a cool, dry place, such as the kitchen counter, or place it unpeeled inside a sealed plastic bag in the crisper drawer of your refrigerator.
- Pickle fresh sliced ginger with vinegar, sugar, and water in equal parts. It will keep in the refrigerator for two months.
- Puree ginger in the food processor, freeze it in ice-cube trays to make blocks of ginger paste and transfer them to an airtight freezer bag.

Oregano

Oregano is a Mediterranean herb; the ancient Greeks called it the "joy of the mountain." This simple but beautiful spiller with its robust flavor and fresh aroma is an embellishment for your garden paths and containers alike.

The herb belongs to the mint family; it is a perennial plant that loves sunshine and warmth.

Benefits

- It offers appetizing flavor to Mediterranean dishes that are based on tomatoes, summer vegetables or eggs.
- Tea extracted from oregano soothes nerves and upset stomachs.
- Fresh oregano is rich in antibacterial and antioxidant properties. It contains fiber, Vitamin K, iron, and calcium.

Planting

Oregano loves sunshine and warm temperatures. Grow your plants outdoors, where there is sun; however, keep them in partial shade during scorching afternoons.

The best time to plant oregano is in spring, six to ten weeks before the last spring frost, when the ambient temperature of the soil should be around 70°F.

Grow oregano from seeds or cuttings using the good quality potting mix for your containers or mixing organic material, such as compost, with garden soil for bedding. Plant them 8–10" apart. Oreganos are spillers and spread about 18".

Once the plants grow to 4", pinch their tops to encourage luxurious growth.

Water oregano thoroughly when the soil feels dry. If the plants are in containers, water until it seeps out of the drainage hole. Mulching prevents the loss of moisture.

Oregano is perennial, meaning it survives winter indoors in colder climates. Trim dead shoots in springtime to allow new growth. Oregano self-seeds and plants are generated from the older ones. Prune plants that are older than three to four years.

Harvesting

Use sharp shears to snip off the stems of mature plants, taking care to leave around two-thirds of the plant intact. Oregano is most palatable in mid-summer, before bolting.

Storing

Oregano is easily stored dried or frozen. Store it in vacuum containers to preserve its freshness.

Comfrey

Comfrey is a hardy perennial, tall with beautiful bell-shaped flowers. This cheerful herb is not only good as a "thriller" but also enriches the soil by bringing up nutrients to the soil's surface. Comfrey leaves have a 17 percent nitrogen content, which is more than other common manures.

Benefits

- The Blocking 14 variants with high potash content make good compost. It is fodder for livestock.
- Comfrey is a companion plant for pears, plums, tomatoes, and other fruits and vegetables.
- When crushed and applied to the skin, comfrey leaves act as cryptic agents, aiding in wound healing and soothing insect bites such as bee stings.
- Brew comfrey tea for stomach upsets, ulcers, and heavy menstrual bleeding.
- It is used as a mouth rinse for gum disease and sore throats.
- Apply a poultice of comfrey roots to a sprained ankle; it will reduce the pain and swelling in no time.

Comfrey has pyrrolizidine alkaloids, mostly concentrated in its roots, and care must be taken while ingesting it. Commercial preparations that use root concentrates may cause liver damage.

Planting

Comfrey grows in cold zones 3–9. In colder zones, it dies in winter and comes back in spring.

It needs sunshine with partial shade. The soil should be well-drained and rich in organic matter with a pH between 6.0–7.0.

They are tall, invasive plants, so space them at least 2' apart.

Comfrey grows best from crowns that are potted first and then bedded. Use a light potting mix in a 6" pot and plant the crowns 3" deep. The plant likes a soil temperature of 50°–60°F and indirect sunlight. Keep the soil moist, but not wet.

When bedding transplants or crown cuttings, plant them 3-8" deep in the soil. Plant them deep in sandy soil in hot weather, but more shallowly in clay soil in cold weather conditions.

Harvest

Harvesting is done in late spring through autumn, when they are about to blot. To make composts just throw the leaves on the garden soil. Microorganisms break them down, to produce soil nutrients.

Fennel

Fennel is a hardy perennial belonging to the carrot family. Inters tingly, it is a vegetable as well as an herb. It is available worldwide. Fennel's shoots, leaves, and seeds are all edible. It has a strong aniseed flavor and is well known for aiding digestion.

Benefits

- Fennel is rich in folates, Vitamin C, Carotene, and fiber. It is good for heart health.
- Due to its Carotene and Vitamin C content, fennel is good for the skin, as well as the mucus membrane that protects organs.
- Its rich flavonoid content gives it anti-inflammatory properties.
- Fennel's low glycemic index and high fiber content, means it helps in blood sugar control and weight management.
- The high folate content of fennel helps to prevent some types of anemia.

Planting

Plant fennel in spring after the last frost. You can grow it from seeds, soaked overnight, directly outdoors or indoors in beds or in pots and containers. However, your growing chances are better when the seeds are sown indoors and then transplanted to the beds later on. Plant them 4–12" apart.

Fennel needs six hours of sunlight every day and well-drained fertile soil that is mixed with organic compost. It can withstand a light frost but not harsh winters and snow.

Water the plants thoroughly when the top of the soil gets dry. About once per fortnight, give them some liquid fertilizer food.

Prevent bolting by pinching off the top of the stems. However, you can allow them to flower if you want to harvest their seeds. The flowers even attract pollinating agents, such as insects and bees!

Harvesting

Harvest fennel regularly by snipping off tiny portions from the top of the stems. The more you trim, the better the foliage is. Do not trim more than one-third of the plant.

Storage

You can keep the stems in a glass of water on your kitchen counter. The leaves stay fresh for three to five days. Some fennel produces bulbs, which can be refrigerated for a week.

Dill

Dill is annual, belonging to the celery family. Grown widely across Eurasia, dill leaves and seeds are used as herbs and spices. Dill's seeds are used in seasoning. The leaves find use in salads, egg dishes, and as a garnish in buttermilk. Fresh dill is more flavorful, with a hint of aniseed and licorice flavors, than dried dill. Bolting alters dill's flavor.

Benefits

- Even a small sprig is sufficient to raise the flavor. Make appetizing salads with dill's small yellow edible flowers.

- Dill has essential oils and finds its application in the cosmetic and pharmaceutical industries.
- Dill seeds have carminative, diuretic, and stomachic properties.

Planting

Dill is sown in mid-spring to mid-summer. It must be sown permanently as it does not like transplantation. Dwarf variants are ideal for container potting and like warm, sunny areas and fertile soil.

Space the plants 6" apart and sow them ½" deep. Press the soil around the plants gently using your hands. For containers, use multipurpose compost and sow them 4" apart.

Water regularly and thoroughly, taking care not to waterlog. Use sticks to support tall plants. Do not grow fennel and dill in the same pot as they cross-breed, producing inferior quality seedlings.

Harvesting

Harvesting is done during the spring and summer seasons. Bolting produces seeds that can be collected in late summer by cutting the stems with the seedheads, and hanging them upside down with the seedheads encased in paper bags. As they dry, they will drop off inside the bag. Grind the seeds or use them whole.

Storage

Hang dill leaves up in dry well-aerated places for a few weeks. When fully dry, bare the stems, and store the leaves in an air-tight container.

Coriander

Coriander, or cilantro, has a characteristically strong, pungent smell. It is widely used in cooking and for medicinal properties. The leaves and seeds are the edible parts of the herb. Well-grown coriander is green and luxurious, spilling out over the container's sides.

Benefits

- Coriander seeds, extracts, and essential oils lower blood sugar in diabetes and raise insulin levels.
- Coriander is a rich source of antioxidants, such as tocopherol, quercetin, and terpinene, with anticancer, immune strengthening, and nerve-protecting properties.
- It acts as a diuretic and can reduce blood pressure, and improve heart health.
- It may help to fight food poisoning infections due to the compound, dodecenal.
- It may promote digestion.

Planting

The herb can be grown indoors, outdoors, on window sills, and on kitchen countertops. Sow the seeds in early spring after the last frost. It thrives well at 17°–27°C. Grow it directly in pots.

Coriander needs direct sunlight and well-drained organically rich soil with a pH of 6.2–6.8. Sow the seeds ½" deep and 6" apart. Press the soil down around the seeds. Cover the top with ½" mulch.

Water the plants regularly and thoroughly.

Germination happens in two to three weeks. Thin out the young plants at 8" apart, as is true for all other herbs. Thinning out the plants allows them to grow to their fullest and also controls the spread of infection.

Since the plant is annual, regular sowing every two to three weeks will ensure a steady supply throughout the season.

Harvesting

Harvest once the plants reach 6" in height. This is optimal for best-tasting leaves. You may allow flowering, to collect seeds for the next season. Harvest the seedheads when they are brown.

Storing

Store seeds and leaves in airtight bags.

Rosemary

A fragrant and evergreen Mediterranean herb, Rosemary belongs to the mint family. Its leaves and the essential oils, extracted from the plant, are used as condiments, for making perfumes and cosmetics and for medicinal properties. It has a wonderfully crisp piney odor.

Benefits

- When applied to the scalp, rosemary, increases blood circulation, improving hair growth.
- Its extract protects the skin from sunburn.
- It may be good for indigestion and fatigue.

Planting

Rosemary grows by propagating stem cuttings from existing plants. Select stems about 2" length and remove leaves from the bottom two third of the cutting. Rosemary grows in the well-drained, loamy soil of pH 6–7. A mixture of perlite and peat moss is best for it.

It needs full sunlight and warm, humid climates. Therefore, it is best to sow rosemary in containers that can be moved indoors during cold winters.

Rosemary does not need much water, and using terracotta pots is preferable. Water thoroughly when the soil is dry to the touch. When kept indoors, ensure six hours of light in a draft-free area.

Harvesting

Trim rosemary regularly to allow gorgeous growth. However, don't trim more than one-third of the plant. Prune just above a leaf joint.

Storage

Dry collected stems are hung upside down in cool, dry places.

Thyme

Thyme, a member of the mint family, is a Mediterranean evergreen with medicinal and culinary properties, and is used in aromatherapy. It thrives in zones 5–9. Its fragrance is surprisingly masculine.

Benefits

- Fights acne.
- Boosts immunity.
- Useful for cough.
- Lowers blood pressure.
- Used as a pesticide.
- Treats yeast infections.
- Uplifts mood.

Planting, Harvesting, and Storage

Place thyme cuttings 12–24" apart, in an area that gets enough sunlight. Sow after the last frost in early spring.

Well-drained fertile soil enriched with organic compost and a pH of 7 is good for thyme. Mulching with limestone gravel facilitates drainage, preventing the rotting of roots.

Water thyme regularly and thoroughly, as soon as the top inch of the soil feels dry to encourage proper growth. Use water-soluble plant food regularly.

Thyme can be grown indoors and in a hydroponic system, where water circulation supplies essential nutrition to the plants. The system has its own grow light, and hence, sunlight is not essential.

Harvesting thyme is just as with any other herb.

Store thyme leaves to use in the winter months. The flavor is most full before bolting and the dried leaves retain the aroma. They can be preserved in vinegar or oil. Thyme leaves in butter enhance the latter's taste.

Chives

Chives belong to the genus, Allium, which includes garlic and onions. This pungent flavored herb is used for culinary and medicinal properties.

Benefits

Chives are rich in nutrients, such as Vitamins K, A, and C, folates, potassium, and calcium. It is low in calories and putting chives in salads can help you cut back on your calorie count.

- The flavonoids in chives have anti-cancer properties. Separate studies found a reduced risk of breast and gastrointestinal cancers with increased use of chives, garlic, and leeks.
- Chives contain choline, which improves mood, memory, and nerve functions.
- It also contains Vitamin K, which is essential for forming blood clots.
- Its folates prevent anemia and improve neural functions.
- Chives reduce inflammation and improve heart health.
- Chive flowers are edible; they taste best when they bloom.

Planting

Chives are perennial herbs with beautiful pink, purple, red, and white flowers that attract butterflies. The leaves and flowers are edible. Chives are good companion plants for celery, carrots, and tomatoes. Two variants, common and garlic chives, are most regularly used.

Chives grow from seeds, during spring and six to eight weeks before the last spring frost. Grow them in a sunny area with partial shade during noon. Chives prefer well-drained organically rich soil.

Germination is best at soil temperatures of 60°–70°F. Chives do not like hot summers.

Since the small bulbs grow near the soil's surface, mulching preserves soil moisture. After bolting, take precautions to check the spread of seeds throughout the garden.

Chives produce well when the plants are divided regularly every three to four years.

Harvesting

Harvest chives one month after they are transplanted or two months after seeding. Harvest three to four times a year, during the first year, and then more frequently.

Cut the leaves at the base.

Storage

Chives are eaten fresh or frozen. Dried chives lose their aroma.

Parsley

Parsley is a Mediterranean herb similar to cilantro but with a milder flavor. Parsley is rich in Vitamin C and iron.

Benefits

- Used in food and beverages as a condiment, garnish, and spice.
- Its essential oil is used in the cosmetic industry to make perfumes, soaps, and cosmetics.
- Parsley prevents urinary bladder infections and kidney stones, and it relieves constipation.

- It allays stomach pain.
- It reduces menstrual spasms and improves flow.

Planting, Harvesting, and Storage

- Parsley is easy to grow in partial shade, in well-drained, rich, and moist soil.
- Sow the seeds directly in potting mix, ½" deep and about 12" apart. Press the soil gently. Water immediately. Once the seedlings appear, thin them to 6" apart.
- You can grow parsley in pots, planting the seeds thinly.
- Water regularly and thoroughly.
- Plants germinate in six weeks.
- Sow parsley in batches to get a continuous supply.
- Bring the plants indoors in harsh winters.
- Bolting occurs during the second year. If you want to preserve the seeds, allow some of the plants to flower.
- Harvesting is easy; cut the stems close to the base. New leaves grow rapidly.
- Storage reduces its flavor.

Sage

Sage is commonly infused to make tea with medicinal properties. It has an earthy flavor.

Benefits

- Sage tea is rich in anti-oxidant rosmarinic acid, carnosol and camphor. It reduces inflammation and is beneficial for diabetes and those with heart disease.
- It is rich in Vitamin K, required for blood clotting.
- Camphor helps to reduce skin aging and sun-induced skin problems.
- Sage tea is good for dental health. It is used in mouthwashes.
- Sage improves brain function, mood, concentration, and memory.
- It can reduce also hot flashes in menopausal women.

Planting

Sage can be sown in or outdoors in spring. Well-drained sandy or loamy soil with slightly acidic pH and at least six hours of sunlight help its growth. Keep in partial shade in very hot areas. Soil temperatures of 60°–70°F and moderately humid conditions are optimal for its growth.

Sage can also be propagated from stem cuttings, by dipping the stem ends in rooting hormones.

Sow saplings at 1.5-2' apart. Water the plants regularly and thoroughly when the top soil feels dry. Sage can be grown in pots 8" in depth.

Harvesting and Storage

Plants are not ready before two and a half months. Harvesting during the first year should be kept to a limit. The flavor is best before bolting. The last harvest should be before the first predicted autumn frost.

The storage of sage's dried leaves is as for other herbs. The flavor is preserved in the dried leaves and is released by crushing them.

Marjoram

A Mediterranean herb, marjoram, has always been famous for its essential oils, with their hundreds of beneficial properties.

Benefits

- It has analgesic, antispasmodic, antibacterial, antiviral, and aphrodisiac properties.
- It is used as a carminative, diuretic, expectorant, sedative, and laxative, etc. It causes sweating.
- It relieves stomach pain.
- It improves nerve function.
- It reduces toothaches, headaches, and body aches. It also relieves muscle spasms and menstrual spasms and improves blood flow.
- Freshen your linen with marjoram oil or lavender oil spray in a cup of water containing ½ teaspoon of baking soda.

Planting, Harvesting, and Storage

Sow marjoram in spring in a pot. Sow plants 12" apart in an organic potting mix—add mulch in the winter months.

Water regularly and thoroughly. Six hours of sunlight, and well-drained soil with pH 6-7, are prerequisites for sweet marjoram. Shift plants indoors in cold climates north of Zone 7.

Harvest leaves one month after sowing. Storage of marjoram leaves is as with other herbs.

Lavender

Lavender, a Mediterranean herb belonging to the mint family, is known for its beautiful flowers, calming aroma, and medicinal properties. It is rich in essential oils, such as pinene, limonene, and linalool, etc.

Benefits

- Lavender is widely used in the cosmetic sector to make soaps, perfumes, and shampoo.
- It may improve skin health, heart health, asthma symptoms, hot flushes, and fight fungal infections.
- Lavender oil is calming and reduces anxiety and depression.

Planting, Harvesting, and Storage

Lavender is a perennial shrub, but you can grow it in containers. It propagates from stem cuttings. You can also plant saplings.

Plant lavender in spring, 12–18" apart in an area with good sunlight and in the well-drained sandy soil of pH 6.7–7.3. Mix compost or organic matter into the soil.

Water only when the top 2" of the soil feels dry. The water-soluble plant feeds and promotes flowering.

Harvest large stems but keep one-third of the plants intact.

Clove

Clove is a native tree of Indonesia, and has always been a favorite in traditional medicine. It was sought-after by medieval spice traders. Its tiny reddish-brown flower buds are dried and used as spices.

Clove has a strong, pungent aroma and is rich in the essential oil eugenol.

Benefits

- Clove oil is antiseptic and aesthetic. It is used in toothache, as germicides, and in mouthwashes.
- Clove is used as a spice in a variety of sweet and savory dishes.

Planting, Harvesting, and Sowing

Cloves grow from seeds. The tree prefers a tropical humid climate. Seeds are planted by laying them directly onto the soil and need not be buried. The plant is a prolific grower, and germination occurs in six weeks. Cloves can be grown in containers, but they will be smaller in size.

A clove tree is fully grown when it is fifteen to twenty years old. These mature trees give the best harvest. However, harvesting can be done after four to six months, when the buds change color from green to slightly pink.

Clove buds can be dried and stored.

Brahmi

Brahmi is a small water-loving perennial creeper that has slender stems with green leaves. It is believed to have originated in India and grows in warm climates all across the globe. It has always been a favorite with Ayurveda physicians.

Benefits

- Brahmi improves memory. It is used in Alzheimer's disease.
- It relieves anxiety.
- It improves irritable bowel syndrome.

Planting, Harvesting, and Storage

Brahmi is easy to grow. You can grow it from store-bought herbs. Cut the stems and place them in some water. Keep in indirect sunlight. Change the water regularly. Roots appear in a week. Plant the saplings in a pot or container.

Brahmi needs little care after it has been successfully planted. Keep the plants in sunlight and water regularly.

Harvest whenever the plants look full. Snip off the leaves and stems with sharp scissors. Use the leaves fresh. You may store them in airtight bags in the refrigerator.

Ashwagandha

Ashwagandha is another powerful medicinal herb. It is a small evergreen shrub with pale green flowers and is believed to have originated in India or Asia. Grow this herb to make your urban homestead one of a kind. All parts of the plant are beneficial. Use the roots to make decoction and tea.

Benefits

- Ashwagandha reduces inflammation.
- It helps to reduce stress and anxiety
- It improves brain function, including memory
- It improves blood sugar.
- It increases energy
- It improves sleep

Planting, Harvesting, and Storage

Plant the seeds of ashwagandha in the summer. They need water, sunlight, and humidity. Sow the seeds 4" apart. The plants appear in a week.

To harvest, loosen the soil around the plants and pull out the whole plant without damaging the soil. Store after drying in airtight containers.

Wormwood

Wormwood belongs to the species artemisia. This ornamental herb is used to garnish beverages.

Benefits

- Wormwood cures intestinal worm infestations.
- It improves digestion.
- It acts like a tonic.
- It is a good companion plant for carrots.

Planting, Harvesting, and Storage

Grow wormwood in the spring. Choose a sunny area to plant the seeds. Spring is the best time to sow. After planting, water the seeds regularly and adequately. Wormwood needs little attention and can be invasive. Prune the herbs regularly.

Harvesting wormwood is done in late summer, after the flowers appear. Cut the branches, wrap them in a paper bag, and hang them upside down to dry the herbs. When fully dry, shake the bunch vigorously for the seeds to drop and collect them in the bag.

Cumin

Cumin is a flowering herb well-known for its dried seeds that are used in cooking and for medicinal properties.

Benefits

- Cumin aids in digestion.
- It prevents food-borne infections.
- It is very rich in minerals, such as iron and potassium.

Planting, Harvesting, and Storage

Cumin plants thrive in well-drained sandy loam soil with a pH of 7–7.5. The plant needs full sunlight for six to eight hours.

Sow cumin seeds indoors two months before the final frost date. Water regularly and adequately. Retain soil moisture and temperature by covering the soil with a plastic wrap. Seeds germinate in two weeks. Once they sprout, keep them in full sunlight.

Cumin must be allowed to flower because the plant is valued for its seeds.

Harvest when the flowers turn brown after about three months. Pluck the flowers, and pick the seed pods. Place them in a paper bag and hang them upside down in a dry place. Roll the dried pods with your hands to release the seeds. Store them in an airtight container.

Shatavari

Shatavari is another herb that will certainly add a new dimension to your homestead. It grows one to two metres tall. Its leaves are pine needle-shaped and green in color. It has hundreds of roots which are dried to make various ayurvedic formulations.

Benefits

- Shatavari is beneficial to female reproductive health. It is used in conditions, such as polycystic ovarian syndrome (PCOS).
- Enhances digestion
- Aids in weight loss
- It has anti-oxidant and anti-viral properties.

Planting, Harvesting, and Storage

Make 6" deep holes in well-drained, organically enriched soil to sow the seeds. Water 1" weekly, but more frequently for a month after sowing. Support the growing plants with stacks. They need sunlight and warm weather conditions.

Harvest the whole plant by digging it out carefully without damaging the roots.

Peel the roots in boiling water and leave them to dry.

Grind the roots to powder and store them in airtight clean bottles.

4

PART 11: PLANTING, HARVESTING, AND STORING

Our natural world has no shortage of beneficial and attractive herbs—plant-scented geraniums and lemon balms to decorate your homes and add value to your family's health.

A FEW MORE

There are geraniums, mint, chamomile, catmints, dandelions, marigolds, and nasturtiums—these beautiful herbs make your homesteading more winsome by attracting pretty pollinators, such as honey bees, colorful ladybugs, and butterflies.

Scented Geraniums

These attractive trees have glands at the base of the leaf hairs, which, when crushed or even touched, release essential oil with an ambrosial scent. Some of the most beautiful variants are apple or chocolate-mint scented, and variegated rose geraniums.

Benefits

- The edible flowers are used in making sweet dishes and jellies.
- Stems and leaves are dried to make potpourri.
- Geranium oil is widely used in alternative medicine for its pain relieving, sedative, antimicrobial, fungicidal, and antispasmodic properties.
- It heals wounds and hemorrhoids and reduces fever and inflammation.

Planting, Harvesting, and Sowing

It is best to buy small nursery plants and sow them in your garden or containers. Use peat-based potting mix for containers. If you have a small garden, use geraniums for landscaping.

Geraniums grow in slightly acidic soil. They love the sun, but partial shade also works for them. They are not fussy about growing, but the potted plants need supervision with food and water. They are often grown as indoor plants, and in winter, some gardeners may hang them, uprooted, indoors in cool, dark places for replanting in spring.

Geraniums are light feeders and easy to maintain. Prune the plant regularly for exuberant growth.

Lemon Balm

An ornamental plant, lemon balm is a Mediterranean herb of the mint family. It is common in temperate climates and is grown as a perennial. The flowers attract pollinating agents, such as honeybees, to your garden.

Benefits

- It has essential oils; geranial, neral and—isomers of citral and other compounds.
- Use as garnishes in salads, soups, sauces, and fillings, and as flavoring agents in candies, liqueurs, and wines. Like most other herbs, add the leaves at the end of the cooking.
- Enjoy a cup of lemon tea in the cold winter evenings; it will take you back to golden summertime.
- The scented oil is used in perfume and cosmetics to make scented shampoos and soaps, etc.
- It has a calming effect on nerves and has gained popularity in aromatherapy.

Planting, Harvesting, and Storage

Clumps of lemon balm are soothing to eyesight; their leaves are dark green and downy. They leave a faint lemon scent on your fingers.

Sow the saplings in deep containers, 20–24" apart, in well-drained, organically enriched soil or in loamy garden soil with a pH of 6–7. Sow the plants where they will get partial shade.

Water the plants adequately and thoroughly when the soil feels dry.

Increase leaf production by adding water-soluble plant food from time to time. When the plants are 6-8" in length, harvest the leaves, leaving at least one-third of the plant intact.

In a garden, lemon balm grows from the seeds of the flowers and, if left unchecked, can overwhelm your patch; so, prune the plants to check overgrowth. Adding mulch to soil prevents seeds from germinating and improves soil nutrients.

Lemon balm loses its fragrance when dried and stored; carry your container indoors to enjoy its freshness in the winter cold.

Mint

A beautiful herb with mint green leaves, mint, a perennial, is common all over the world. Mint has essential oils in the leaves and stems. The leaves have a sweet fragrance and cool, sweet taste. Peppermint has a menthol-like aftertaste.

Benefits

- Mint is very rich in Vitamin A (1/2 ounce of spearmint has 12 percent RDI, or recommended dietary allowance of the vitamin), iron (9 percent RDI), folate (4 percent RDI), and manganese (8 percent RDI). Vitamin A is essential for eyesight, night vision, and skin health.
- Mint is rich in antioxidants that can protect organs from decay and damage.
- Mint can improve digestion and irritable bowel syndrome,
- Mint may improve brain function.
- Mint fights bad breath.
- Peppermint and spearmint are used as food flavoring agents.

Planting, Harvesting, and Storage

Mint is difficult to grow from seeds. Either buy saplings from a nursery or use cuttings from a healthy plant. A 4" sprig, placed in a glass of water, will give out roots within a week. Once the roots are lengthened, transplant them into the soil. Mint can also be propagated by runners. If your neighbor or friends have mint, you can borrow runners from them to grow your own plants.

Plant mint plants 6" apart in well-drained, moist, organically enriched rich soil of pH 6–7 in a deep container. Keep the soil moist, and keep the plant on a windowsill or a position where it will get enough sunlight.

If you plan to plant mint in the garden, grow it in a big container that you submerge underneath the soil, with its rim above the surface level, or in a raised bed. This prevents mint from rampant propagation throughout your garden.

Trim your plants often to give them a good shape. Clipping off the flowers will prolong the harvesting season. After that, you should divide your plants every two to three years.

Harvest from late spring through to early autumn. Pinch off small sections of the stems with the leaves still attached to them, but keep one-third of the plants intact.

Mint dies in winter but reappears in spring. Add mulch during the winter months to protect its roots.

You can store mint leaves by hanging the stems upside down. When they are crisp, shave the leaves off the stems and collect them in Ziploc bags.

Chamomile

Chamomile is an herb that belongs to the daisy-like flowers of the Asteraceae family. Chamomile has been known to soothe anxiety and induce sleep since ancient times. There are two varieties, Roman and German. They both have the same medicinal values and are grown in a similar manner.

Benefits

- Apigenin, an antioxidant in chamomile, induces sleep. It has been found to reduce depressive symptoms in postmenopausal women and to improve sleep quality. Chamomile tea before bedtime may help you to sleep better, with fewer nighttime awakenings.
- Chamomile can aid in digestion.
- Apigenin can protect against some cancers of the breast, uterus, prostate, skin, thyroid, and digestive tract.
- It can improve heart health and reduce blood sugar in diabetics.
- The sweet fragrant herb is a good companion plant for cruciform vegetables, onions, and cucumbers.
- The flowers attract bees and butterflies to your garden.

Planting, Harvesting, and Storage

Chamomile is easy to grow from plants, divisions, or seeds in beds and containers. Plant chamomile plants 8" apart in sunny spots. Use well-drained, dry, and fertile soil mixed with organic matter or compost. Water immediately after planting; add an inch of water per week until the roots take hold.

Add a small supply of continuous-release fertilizer during planting and replenish it regularly during growth. This helps to induce substantial plant growth. Use sticks and supports to help the plant grow.

Mulching prevents drying up the soil.

Flowers are harvested after blooming; pinch them off below the flower heads.

Chamomile flowers can be used fresh or dried. Dry them by spreading them out on a screen in dry and dark places, then store them in airtight containers.

Nasturtium

Grow these flaming yellow and red flowers in your herbal garden to throw in a lot of cheer and boldness. They grow profusely in containers and beds, and attract honeybees for pollination. They are also good companion plants to melon, pumpkins, beans, broccoli, and a host of other vegetables. They are of two types; trailing and bush. Choose them according to your garden type. Trailing varieties look gorgeous in hanging baskets and window boxes.

Benefits

- Almost all parts of the plant are edible. Leaves, flowers, and seedpods have a peppery flavor and can be used as garnishes.
- Nasturtium is rich in Vitamin C; its vitamin content is similar to parsley.
- It is rich in antioxidants and has antifungal and antibacterial properties.

Planting, Harvesting, and Storage

If you want to plant nasturtiums indoors, sow the seeds two to four weeks before the last spring frost date. For an outdoor garden, sow seeds one to two weeks after spring's final frost. Nasturtiums are not fussy and grow easily on ordinary, but well-drained soils. Too much nitrogen fertilizer promotes leaf growth instead of flowers. Soil temperature should be between 55°–65°F.

Keep nasturtiums in the bright sunlight for colorful flowers.

Water regularly and thoroughly during the growing season.

Pinch off dead flowers to promote further flowering.

Nasturtiums' leaves and flowers can be harvested once they bloom. Harvest the seed pods before they harden. Harvest flowers, pods, and leaves using scissors to prevent plant damage. A few mature seed pods can be collected to glean seeds for the next season.

Turmeric

Turmeric, an essential spice in South Asian cooking, is an herb that has been used since the olden days for its healing properties. It was also used as a natural dye for improving skin complexion and blemishes.

The herb is annual, and belongs to the ginger family. It has a pungent taste.

It has many benefits that are already scientifically proven.

Benefits

- Curcumin, turmeric's essential compound, has potent anti-inflammatory, antioxidant, and antibacterial properties. To improve its bioavailability, consume turmeric with black pepper which increases curcumin absorption by 2,000 percent (Shoba et al., 1998). Fats and oils in cooking also improve its absorption.
- Turmeric's anti-inflammatory properties make it useful for heart health and for checking various degenerative diseases, such as cancer and diabetes. Turmeric acts as a wonder in sprains and joint swelling due to minor trauma.

- Turmeric acts as an antiseptic; it is used in hospitals for wound dressing and to reduce hand swelling after intravenous drips have been administered.
- Turmeric is used as a spice in cooking; it renders a distinct flavor to curry and gives it a good color.
- Turmeric paste improves the skin's complexion and reduces the blemishes of acne. It helps to reduce pain and swelling in burns and insect bites. However, like other herbal products, the patient must be tested for allergy before a topical application.

But how can you grow turmeric in urban homesteading? Is it possible that the golden herb can grow in your zone and in containers?

Planting, Harvesting, and Storage

Turmeric grows from rhizomes. Harvested turmeric has a cluster of rhizomes around a central node.

You can buy certified organic rhizomes from stores. Once you harvest your crops, you can store the seeds for future use.

Turmeric is native to India; it needs sun and water. It has a long growing period that lasts for eight to ten months. This period should be frost-free. The trick is to plant turmeric in winter and harvest it in fall.

In Zones 8 and above, choose an outdoor location to plant it. In lower zones, you can grow the plant indoors, where there is a good amount of sunlight.

If you want to grow turmeric in containers, choose bigger and deeper ones than you would normally use for herbs.

Soil should be well-drained and loose. For containers, mix 20-30 percent of compost with 70-80 percent of organic compost. Do not use fresh manure. Any subsequent feeds should be water-soluble plant food.

Plant rhizomes 2-4" deep, and 4-6" apart. Just as with garlic and ginger, make holes in the soil with your finger and plant the rhizomes with their small fingers or nubs facing upwards. Keep the containers in warm areas, and not much sunlight is needed before sprouting.

Water when the soil feels dry.

Sprouting may happen faster indoors than in beds. Once sprouts appear, give them adequate sunlight, water, and food.

Stop watering close to harvest time.

After eight to ten months, when the leaves turn yellow, it is time for harvesting. Carefully dig the soil around the plants with a trowel, taking care not to damage them.

Once the soil is loose enough, pull the plants gently out by their stalks.

Clean the rhizomes and air dry before storage.

Bay Laurel

Bay laurel is an evergreen shrub. Its long leaves are decorative and were used by ancient Greeks to make crowns of victory wreaths.

During the Renaissance period, doctors were presented with branches and berries of bay laurel after graduation, hence the origin of the term "baccalaureate" (bacca lauri: laurel berry—the symbol of victory).

The leaves release a distinct aroma making laurel an invaluable addition to many sweet and savory dishes. You can grow it in containers or beds. However, its leaves are toxic to cats, dogs, and horses.

Benefits

- Bay leaves, fresh or dried, are added to various sweet and savory dishes.
- As with insecticides and bug repellents, bay leaves can be placed inside food grain canisters, as they protect other plants from undesirable insects.
- Throw a few pieces of laurel wood onto your grill to give a pleasant aroma to the roasted food.

Planting, Harvesting, and Storage

Bay laurel is an ornamental evergreen. It can grow to be very tall and is usually kept trimmed to 2-5' high. You can even grow it in containers.

Bay laurel grows well in Zones 8 and above, in well-drained, organically rich soil. Use cuttings, transplants, or seeds to grow your plant.

For garden soil, one part of sand or finely crushed gravel mixed with six parts of enriched soil is used.

Change the container and replenish the soil every three years, using mature compost for the top layer. Add small quantities of fertilizer fortnightly for outdoor and monthly for indoor plants.

During the freezing winter months, keep the containers indoors and protect the roots with sacks or wraps. They will still need sunlight. Keep your plant pruned to get the best results.

Mature bay leaves are better in flavor than young fresh leaves. They can be dried and stored in airtight containers or Ziploc bags.

Catmint

Unlike catnip, catmint does not attract cats. This aromatic herb with its attractive lavender flowers is used for landscaping.

Benefits

- Catmint is a natural insect repellent and is beneficial to your vegetable patch.
- Use it to complement your roses.
- Catmint tea is calming and relieves throat congestion and menstrual cramps.
- You can use the leaves as garnish and condiments for soups and sauces.

Planting

Catmint, like catnip, belongs to the mint family. The perennial plants grow extensively and easily, even in Zone 4 weather conditions. Use them as edges or runners along your garden path; they are magnificent "spillers." They need sunlight with partial shade and well-drained organic soil. Newer variants of catmint are always coming up, choose the ones that best suit your garden. You can buy new plants or use cuttings or divisions of mother plants.

In the first week, the saplings need alternate day watering, which can be reduced to once a week for another month. Catmints, especially the "Sweet Dreams" variety, tolerate drought conditions and are not heavy feeders.

The "Six Hills Giant" variety with lavender flowers is the tallest and requires spacing while planting. "Little Titch" does not need much spacing and is good for containers.

Lemon Verbena

Of all the citrusy flavors, lemon verbena with its maximum oil concentration, is undoubtedly the natural choice for bakers, who love it for its zesty flavor. It is intensely floral but not bitter, differing from its family member, lemongrass, which comes with a more astringent tang.

Benefits

- Infuse sauce, tea, and oil, etc. with whole leaves if you like lemon flavor.
- Season your poultry dishes, soups, and salsa. Make ice creams, tarts, and jellies with verbena's natural lemon flavor.
- Lemon verbena is said to relieve indigestion, constipation, cough, joint pains, and fever.

Planting

Lemon verbena is a sturdy perennial that tolerates cold zones. True to its mint nature, it grows easily and, if unchecked, can become invasive. It likes the sun with partial shade and is best pruned in early spring to give it a fuller look.

You can grow lemon verbena in containers that have multiple holes to drain out the excess water. Use loose potting mixes with mature compost and keep the container in sunlight. Water regularly. Lemon verbena goes into a dormant stage when temperatures drop to 40°F. Keep the containers indoors. You may cut the plants down to the soil level, cover them with soil, and add layers of mulch to prevent winter frost.

Harvesting

The leaves are best during the flowering season. To harvest them cut the stems within ¼" of a leaf or a node so that the stem grows back from the cut section.

Celery

If you have tasted garden-grown celery, you will not like store-bought celery anymore. This humble herb (which doubles up as a vegetable) belongs to the family Apiaceae, which includes coriander, parsley, and fennel.

Benefits

- It is widely used in Cajun and Creole cooking, with bell peppers and onions.
- If you are fond of detox juice, celery is your natural choice.
- It is rich in Vitamins C and K, folates, and potassium.

Planting, Harvesting, and Storage

Sow seeds indoors eight to ten weeks before the last frost. It is a biennial plant, and if you want a year-round supply, plant it twice, during May – June and September – October.

Make small holes in loose soil to house two to three seeds of celery. Do not cover the seeds with soil; they need direct exposure to sunlight. In the absence of sunlight, a growth light should be used to germinate the seeds.

Keep the seeds moist by spray misting them with water regularly. In a cold zone, cover the tray with plastic wrap to retain its humidity. Remove the wrap once the first shoots appear. Germination may take more than two weeks.

Transplant the plants, spacing them 12" apart in organically enriched soil of pH 6.5-7.5, and temperature 50°F.

Feed growing celery monthly.

Grow your celery, lettuce, coriander, and chives from store-bought ones. Cut them near their bases leaving generous portions of green stalk. The roots should be intact. Keep these sections in a bowl of water, with the roots submerged and the stalks facing up. Expose them to sunlight. Green leaves will appear after about a week. Transplant the whole plant into loose moist soil, keeping the leaves above the soil's surface. Water the plants. It is fascinating to watch as new stalks appear from the base.

You can pile up soil around the base of the stalks, once they double in size. This procedure, called blanching, reduces the bitterness of celery.

Harvest celery four months after sowing, once the stalks are about 6" in length.

Store unused celery in plastic bags for up to two weeks in the crisp section of your refrigerator. Remove the leaves for better results.

To store for winter, cut the stalks, blanch them in boiling water for a minute, then throw them in iced water. Remove and pat dry. Keep in an airtight freezer bag and refrigerate.

Stevia

Stevia or candy leaf, a flowering plant of the Aster family, is grown for its sweet leaves—a substitute for chemically processed sugar. The plant is native to Paraguay.

Benefits

- Stevia's sweetness stems from several sweet-tasting sugars in the leaves, called steviol glycosides. Since antiquity, leaves have been used as sweeteners. Their property was discovered by the world at large relatively recently, and they are processed by giant pharmaceutical companies to produce non-caloric sugars. A single stevia tablet is three hundred times sweeter than table sugar and is devoid of calories, carbohydrates, and chemicals.
- Stevia can lower bad cholesterol or LDL and increase good cholesterol or HDL.
- Infuse the leaves in tea to avoid chemical sugar.

Planting, Harvesting, Storage

You can grow stevia from seeds or stem cuttings. They can be grown completely indoors in containers or transplanted later in the garden.

The plants need at least six hours of sunlight.

Grow Stevia in a potting mix that is rich in organic matter. Avoid chemical fertilizers to get better-tasting leaves. Sow the plants ½" deep and 3" apart. Water immediately after sowing. Keep the soil uniformly moist during germination. Once the plants appear, thin them out, keeping two to three plants in one large container. To transplant them into the garden, leave a minimum distance of 18" between each plant to allow fuller growth.

Water your plants regularly, and remember that bolting diminishes the taste of the leaves. Snip off the flower buds, trim the stems, and prune the plants for more luxurious growth.

For USDA hardiness Zones lower than 8, keep the stevia plants indoors during winter. The plants in the garden can be protected by several layers of mulch on the topsoil.

To harvest the leaves, just snip them off, and use them, fresh or dried, in your dessert items or beverages. Dried leaves can be stored in airtight containers in the refrigerator for months.

Tagetes

Want a cheerful spot in your garden? Consider tagetes. Tagetes is related to the bright flower, marigold. They are herbs belonging to the Aster family and are native to Mexico.

Benefits

- Bright flowering tagetes are great companions to tomatoes, eggplant, and potatoes, etc. However, avoid planting them near legumes.
- They are good attractors of pollinating agents, such as butterflies, honeybees, and colorful ladybugs.
- Their essential oil extract, called tagete or marigold oil, is used in the cosmetic and culinary sectors. It is also the source of some food colors.
- The juice of tagete can eradicate intestinal worms.
- They are one of the most common edible flowers worldwide.
- Crushed leaves stop bleeding from cuts and abrasions wonderfully. Their healing property can be compared to some topical antibiotic preparations.

Planting, Harvesting, and Storage

Planting tagetes is easy; they grow in most soils and are drought-resistant.

Sow the seeds outdoors, 12-30" apart, a few weeks before the last frost. Keep them covered to preserve humidity. Soil temperature should be 70°F, pH 6-7.

The plants need direct sunlight, with some shade during noon in hot zones. Water them regularly, and give them water-soluble plant food monthly.

Remove the dead flower heads to prolong the flowering season.

Harvest mature flowers. Dried flower heads, when broken apart, release seeds. The seeds can be collected and used for next season, but chances are they will give a different color variety. This is because of the rampant hybridization of the marigolds.

Aloe Vera

Aloe is derived from the Arabic word "Alloeh," meaning shining bitter substance, while vera means true. The Greeks considered aloe a panacea, that is, a cure for all ailments. The plant has succulent leaves that form a compact rosette.

Benefits

- Aloe vera tooth gel can fight cavities. Its anthraquinone compounds are anti-inflammatory and promote healing.
- Aloe latex can treat constipation.
- Aloe gel can heal diabetic foot ulcers.

- Leaf extracts can be used in superficial cuts and burns for anti-microbial and anti-oxidant properties.
- It may protect the skin from sunburn.

Planting, harvesting, Storage

Plant aloe in some cactus potting or regular garden soil mixed with perlite or sand. The pot must have several drainage holes. Let the soil become completely dry before you water the plants. Aloe vera does not need much food; once a year, an application of a phosphorus-based liquid plant food at half-strength is sufficient for proper growth.

Keep the plants in sunlight. You will have to wait for a year to harvest the leaves.

To harvest, select the thicker leaves, ensuring they are healthy. Cut them at their bases (this is where their beneficial compounds are concentrated), then wash and dry them. Collect the sap for latex. Slit the leaves with a knife and extract the gel. Fresh aloe gel can be directly applied to the skin as an emollient and moisturizer. You can store it in clean jars and refrigerate it for future use. If it clumps, run it through a blender, and then strain, and bottle.

To make aloe juice, add about two tablespoons of the gel to a cup of any liquid.

Valerian

Valerian is considered "nature's valium," and many have known of its ability to induce sleep since the olden days.

Benefits

- Valerian has a calming effect on agitated nerves.
- It is used in anxiety to enable sleep.
- It can be used in restless leg syndrome.
- It may relieve menstrual conditions, such as premenstrual tension and hot flashes.
- Its roots and rhizomes are used for dietary supplements, tea, and for making tinctures.

Planting, Harvesting, and Storage

Valerian is a perennial plant.

It can be grown from cuttings or seeds in moist soil. It needs sunlight. The flower stalks are tall, so in your garden, plant them at the back.

Harvest the roots of a mature two-year-old plant. The roots have an unpleasant odor. Do not use them unsupervised for any long duration.

Fenugreek

Fenugreek is an herb that is well-known for its medicinal property. It is also used in South Asian cuisine as a spice.

Benefits

- Fenugreek lowers blood sugar and is a known hypoglycemic agent. It reduces the concurrent use of diabetic medications.
- It has good fiber content and can reduce cholesterol levels in the blood.
- It may have beneficial effects on libido.
- The leaves are eaten fried with vegetables or are added to unleavened bread.

Planting, Harvesting, and Storage

Growing fenugreek is easy in pots and containers. It does not require deep pots. Grow the plants from good healthy seeds. Soak the seeds overnight before sowing them in warm moist, organically enriched soil. Fenugreek must be planted and grown in the same pot.

Water regularly. The plants will be ready for harvesting in about a month's time.

Harvest no more than one-third of the plants, which will regrow from the cut areas. Bolting prolongs harvesting.

If you want to gather the seeds, you will need to wait three to five months. Seeds form inside pods. Collect and dry the seeds for future use.

You can also make powder out of the seeds for future purposes.

Garlic

Garlic, like chives and onions, belongs to the genus Allium. People have used it since ancient times to enhance the gastronomic flavors of cooked dishes, and it is well-known for its medicinal value. Some believe that the ancient Olympic athletes were given garlic to improve their performance. The father of Western medicine, Hippocrates, used garlic to cure various ailments and to promote health.

Benefits

- Garlic reduces high cholesterol and blood pressure and improves heart health.
- It has strong anti-cancer properties and may protect against some brain, lung, prostate, and colon cancers.
- Its anti-inflammatory properties are good for relieving bone pains.
- Garlic has diallyl sulfide, a compound a hundred times more powerful against some microbes than antibiotics.

Planting

There are two varieties of garlic, Softneck, and Hardneck. The latter has a stronger taste, is suitable for colder regions, and is harvested earlier. The Softneck varieties have better storage. They are often plaited and hung in the kitchen larder.

Break down the garlic into individual cloves. Sow the cloves separately with their tips showing above the soil in well-drained, organically enriched, moist soil. Sow them 6" apart, with 12" between two rows. Cover the pots with light linen or a cloche to prevent the birds from eating the cloves.

Water the cloves regularly until bulbs appear. The stalks, called scapes, appear soon after, and removing them increases the bulb size.

Harvesting and Storage

Add some leaves to salads, taking care not to attenuate plant growth. June through August is the best harvesting season. Experts say harvesting is best before the leaves turn yellow. Dig out the garlic from the soil gently.

Garlic is easy to store. It keeps well in dark, cool places. You can peel the cloves and store them in the refrigerator.

Catnip

Catnip is an herb belonging to the mint family.

Benefits

- Catnip's flowering tops are used as medicines.
- It makes insecticides and pesticides.
- The leaves are used for seasoning dishes and as a medicinal tea to relieve cold.
- Cat toys are stuffed with catnips. Cats love to roll and rub against catnip bushes.

Planting and Harvesting

Catnips are perennial, but they die in winter to return in spring. They can be grown indoors and outdoors and rotated according to weather conditions.

Plant catnips in spring, after frost, in well-drained, organically rich soil. Sow the plants 18–24" apart. Keep them in sunny areas with partial shade at noon. Water them judiciously and add liquid plant food regularly.

Leaves are ready to harvest when the plant grows to 6-8" in length.

Tarragon

Tarragon is a Mediterranean herb known for its bittersweet flavor, similar to licorice. It belongs to the sunflower family.

Benefits

- Tarragon is used in cooking meat, fish, poultry, and soups for its delicate taste.
- It is rich in manganese, a micronutrient essential for bone health, growth, and metabolism.
- Its potassium content is good for heart, muscle, and nerve functions.
- It may improve appetite.
- It has a calming effect and induces sleep.

Planting and Harvesting

A perennial plant, tarragon grows in sunny areas. Two common varieties are French and Russian; the former tastes better than the Russian variety.

It grows from cuttings or root division. You can also buy saplings and sow in fertile, well-drained soil.

Growing and harvesting tarragon is as with the other herbs; its leaves can be frozen. They can be dried and stored. A vinegar extract of tarragon keeps for a longer time.

Curry

Curry is an herb grown both for decorative and household purposes. A fully grown plant is eye-catching with its luxurious green foliage covers. It also has a unique aroma and flavor and is a common ingredient in South Asian cuisine.

Benefits

- Curry leaves are rich sources of antioxidants, such as mahanimbine, linalool, and myrcene, etc.
- Curry leaves may protect the heart, nerves, and brain and may have anti-cancer properties.
- They are anti-inflammatory, analgesic, and antibacterial.
- As a garnish, curry leaves are added to vegetarian and non-vegetarian dishes.

Planting, Harvesting, and Storage

Curry is native to India. It is easy to grow it from seeds or cuttings. Seeds must be soaked before sowing them in the soil.

You can grow curry anywhere, in pots, buckets, indoors, or outdoors; it only needs well-drained soil, mixed with organic compost and sand. Keep the newly sown plants in milder sunlight. Check soil moisture daily and water the soil thoroughly when it feels dry. You will need to add a water-based plant food – neem, or mustard biowastes – to replenish the soil's nutrients.

The plant is perennial and is soon ready for a bountiful harvest.

Curry leaves can be stored frozen in air-tight bags.

Elderberries

Black elderberries are used for their medicinal properties. Elderberries are perennial, and once planted do not need much care.

Benefits

- The berries are loaded with antioxidants and anti-inflammatory agents.
- They are used to relieve symptoms of flu.
- They are used to relieve joint and muscle pains.
- They are used to treat constipation.

Planting, Harvesting, And Storage

Elderberry is hardy and thrives in all sorts of weather conditions. Choose a plant that looks healthy and plant it in an open area that gets lots of sunshine. The soil must be well-drained, and moist soil.

Elderberries need 1" of water per week.; but a growing plant needs more.

The surrounding area must be kept free of weeds, and a space of 6–8' must be kept between two plants. Apply 3" of mulch to check weeds.

Use a nitrogen-rich fertilizer for the growing plant. Older plants need less nitrogen.

Harvesting flowers and berries by snipping them off the branches. Harvest the flowers in full bloom. Leave some behind for fruiting.

Prune the plant regularly.

Store elderberries in a cool, dark place at temperatures 68°F–70°F. Keep them away from children and pets.

PEST CONTROL, AND FERTILIZERS

C rop production works best with optimal soil nutrients. Herbs, fortunately, are not heavy feeders, but they do need food while germinating.

You can enrich garden soil by adding fertilizers. Chemical fertilizers are readily available in the market. However, for your homesteading, you would probably like to get personally involved every step of the way, and making your own fertilizer seems a natural choice.

GARDENING AND EFFECTS ON CLIMATE CHANGE

Composting recycled materials and food waste provide organic and natural nutrients to the soil. There also are other benefits. Composting an acre of soil can clean almost 75 percent of a car's annual emissions. It reduces dependence on fossil-fuel-based fertilizers, improves soil resilience, and incorporates carbon into the soil.

Composting

Composting gives plants organic nourishment and reduces the burden on urban landfills where waste is burnt, releasing methane gas, a powerful global warming agent.

The Things You Can Compost

Compost needs three basic ingredients: browns, such as twigs, cardboard pieces, untreated sawdust or wood pieces; greens, such as grass bits, leaves, vegetable peels; and water to form the compost. The browns give nitrogen and the greens return carbon to the soil. Alternate different layers to make the compost, keeping the proportions of browns and greens equal.

You can use:

- Vegetable peel, fruit peel, and scraps
- Eggshells
- Coffee grounds and tea bags
- Shells from nuts
- Shredded newspaper and cardboard
- Paper pieces
- Bits of grass and yard scraps
- Leaves and the remnants of plants
- Hay or straw
- Untreated wood and sawdust

- Hair and fur, and nail clippings without nail polish
- Ashes from a fireplace

The Things You Cannot Compost

- Coal or charcoal ash with harmful material for the plants.
- Dairy and poultry, emits foul odors and attract flies and rodents.
- Fats, lard, grease, meat, fish scraps, or bones.
- Avoid pet litter and feces. It attracts parasites, harmful bacteria, and other pathogens.
- Yard trimmings with *pesticides* or *treated* wood.
- Ensure the materials used are healthy and free from mold, insects, and chemicals. Some plants, such as black walnut leaves and bark, are toxic to the soil.

How to Compost

Only a few basic tools are needed to make compost, including a pitchfork, a shovel, a bin, and a water sprinkler. Select a shady corner to make the compost.

Add the browns and the greens, taking care to shred and chop them into smaller pieces. If the content is dry, add some water and mix them well. The fruit and vegetable scraps should remain covered underneath the pile. Leave it like this for two months, although sometimes it can take up to two years to form compost, depending on the temperature. Compost must be turned regularly and mixed with water to help the decomposition of its components. Alternately, cover the mass with a tarpaulin to retain moisture.

For most of our urban households, we may not have the bonus of a backyard. Instead, you can purchase a compost bin from the local hardware shop.

Grab this opportunity to teach your children what materials can go into compost so as not to attract vermin and flies while returning soil nutrition. When done properly, it does not smell or attract rodents into the house.

Vermicomposter

A vermicomposter is a composter that uses worms. The worms break down food scraps and enrich the soil with their excreta, called "castings". It is easy to make vermicompost indoors for an urban homestead.

What is the benefit of vermicompost?

Vermicompost improves drainage, retains moisture, and is an excellent organic nitrogen source.

While vermicomposting, the bin must be kept in a shady area with moderate temperatures, such as under the kitchen sink, in the garage, or in the basement. For outdoor bins, keep them in shady spots and cover them during the day.

Vermicompost uses fruit and vegetable scraps, tea bags, and coffee grounds, but not coffee filters. Do not add offal or dairy products as they can attract flies and rodents.

Worms cannot break down plastics or browns.

Throw away any liquid that collects under the bin, and once the compost is fully formed, feed the worms on one side of the bin while gathering the compost from the other side.

Vermicomposting is labor-intensive but yields nutrient-dense material. Reserve it for outdoor plants. For indoor plants, a little of it greatly benefits their growth.

Pest Control

Perhaps due to their medicinal properties, most herbs are resistant to pests. But even so, they are sometimes plagued by tenacious bugs, such as aphids, caterpillars, and beetles. Instead of using harsh chemical pesticides, we can use more friendly methods to protect our green companions.

The truth is, we can let nature take its course. The use of natural agents to control pests is called "biological control." The praying mantis eats many insects, and birds, such as orioles, bluebirds, cardinals, and others, eat slugs, snails, cabbage worms, whiteflies, moths, aphids, and other pests. Even honey bees and wasps keep herbs free of pests; wasps avoid humans unless they use strong perfume.

Other microscopic organisms in the soil can be excellent pesticides, as well. One such organism is nematodes, belonging to the family Steinernematidae and Heterorhabditidae. They are indigenous to the soil and feed on the larval forms of fleas, beetles, ants, and termites, considerably decreasing the presence of adult bugs. It is helpful to know which pests to control, their life cycles, and the particular nematode species that will kill them.

For more persistent bugs, such as beetles, the ubiquitous dish soap can come in handy. Dissolve a tablespoon of dish soap in a quart of water and spray your herbs well from the top down, taking care to bathe the whole plant with the soap solution.

The plant kingdom is also rich in beneficial components, many of which have intrinsic healing properties. Watching a tree heal itself is wonderful, and of all the trees, the neem tree stands out for its healing properties. In homesteading, neem oil is your most trusted ally.

Keep a spray bottle with half-diluted neem water handy. Shake the solution well before applying it to your herbs. This simple organic spray will kill most harmful insects.

Make it fresh once a week.

With its strong scent and potent essential oils, cedar oil also disperses the most persistent bugs, including fleas and ticks. Other oils with similar benefits are citronella, garlic, orange, lemongrass, tea tree oil, lavender, and peppermint oil.

Add a few drops of any of these oils to about a cup of water. Change the solution frequently for effectiveness. Do not forget to shake the bottle well before use.

Wash your herbs thoroughly before consumption.

Plants, such as coriander, chives, garlic, lavender, mint, and oregano are among many companion plants that protect other plants from pests. Coriander and dill kill aphids and spider mites; lavender checks mosquitoes, fleas, flies, and moths; basil is repellent for moths and flies; Alliums check cabbage worms, aphids, and carrot flies, among others.

Disease Control

It is good to know what infestations we should be careful about, because the proverb "a stitch in time saves nine" is truly applicable to homesteading.

Aphids

These insects love new foliage. Their sticky secretion (called honeydew) attracts sooty molds and ants and can disfigure the plant, causing the leaves to curl up. Herbs that grow rapidly and profusely tend to attract aphids.

To treat a plant with aphids, use horticulture soaps and neem oil.

Spider Mites

These can destroy plants and are very difficult to identify; fine web-like structures mean hundreds of these tiny arachnids have already infested the leaves.

Bronze-like or shiny leaf discoloration means a particularly heavy infestation.

To detect mite infestation, look for stippling on the leaves and webbing underneath. Soak some soap and rubbing alcohol solution in water, and with a cloth, wipe down the leaves thoroughly, taking care of getting into the corners and folds. For smaller plants, spray mist the solution.

Whiteflies

Whiteflies cling to the under-surfaces of leaves. Like aphids, they release a sticky honeydew secretion while sucking out the plant's juices, and attracting molds and ants.

Use a soap-water solution to help get rid of these pests.

Leafminers

These are the larvae of moths, sawflies, beetles, or flies. They live inside the leaves, leaving behind trails as they eat.

A homemade solution of one teaspoon of baking soda, dish soap, and a cup of water can check these leaf eaters.

Parsley Worms

Birds do not eat these bad-tasting caterpillars, which are found on parsley and dill. They are striking and morph into beautiful swallowtail butterflies.

Flea Beetles

They do not cause much damage except for chewing tiny holes in the leaves.

Weevils and Spittle Bugs

Weevils are like flea beetles on parsley, but do not cause serious harm. Simply wash them off the leaves.

However, be aware that excess watering causes fungal infections such as root rot, caused by fusarium species. Common fungal infestations cause black spots on the upper surface of the leaves, rust spots on the undersides, moldiness of blight, and powdery white mildew that looks like baby powder. Soon the leaves turn yellow, limp, and fall off.

To get rid of it, make a solution of 1 tablespoon of baking soda, 1 tablespoon of oil, and 1 teaspoon of dish soap in a gallon of water. Use this solution to spray your plants.

Alternatively, using 2 tablespoons of vinegar in a gallon of water, and neem oil is also effective.

To prevent fungal infections, take the following precautions:

- Choose plants that are healthy and disease-free. They should match your environment and climate.
- Select the correct places for them to grow, ensuring sunlight and air.
- Plant them thinly.
- Water your plants early in the morning to avoid soaking the soil. Watering near the soil prevents wetness in the leaves that may attract fungus. Avoid overwatering at all costs.
- Mulching your topsoil prevents leaves from contacting the soil.
- Prune your herbs to prevent fungal growth, using clean implements.

The Best Fertilizers for Herbs

Some herbs are sparse eaters, while others need a little more food. The first category of plants includes most Mediterranean herbs, such as lavender, mint, marjoram, oregano, and rosemary. They are usually perennials; slow-growing with small leaves or needles and stiff stems.

Sometimes we want to increase the growth of our plants and herbs, but for certain delicate plants, such as rosemary, this can reduce the essential oils they produce. This is especially true in the Mediterranean species (Hassani, 2019).

Plants, belonging to the latter category, are usually rapid growers with larger leaves. They are annuals such as basil, coriander, and dill; bi-annuals, are plants such as parsley, and perennials are plants such as chives.

Which fertilizers are best for our urban homestead? In this book, we will discuss organic fertilizers to restore vigor to the soil and ensure health for your herbs.

The type of fertilizer you use often depends on the nature of the planting soil. In sandy soil, slow-release fertilizers with equal amounts of nitrogen, phosphorus, and potassium work best for herbs. For faster-growing plants, organic fertilizer, such as fish emulsion, which is naturally rich in nitrogen and has an NPK ratio of 4-1-1 or 5-1-1, is best.

How frequently should the plants feed? For normal soil conditions, adding fertilizer once at the beginning of spring, when the plants come back from dormancy or at the beginning of the growing season, is sufficient.

If the leaves turn yellow, it may indicate a nitrogen deficiency. However, it can also be due to fungal infestation. therefore, before adding a nitrogen-enriched solution, it would be wise to check for leaf infections.

Plants in containers may need more frequent applications of fertilizer because of soil and nutrient seepage, due to the more frequent watering. Use organic fertilizers fortnightly. Water-based plant foods of the slow-release type may need less frequent applications.

Use a hydroponic fertilizer for hydroponic herbs. Yellow leaves may indicate a magnesium deficiency. Use suitable magnesium and calcium-based hydroponic fertilizers based on the instruction manuals.

Choosing Fertilizers for Your Herbs

An ideal fertilizer should not only provide nourishment to your herbs but should also facilitate the growth of helpful microorganisms and improve the soil's texture.

Synthetic fertilizers act quickly, supplying essential nutrients to plants in high amounts. However, they do not promote the growth of helpful microbes, raise soil salinity and diminish soil texture. They do not return carbon to the soil. Conversely, organic fertilizers are entirely natural, but are comparatively slow-acting, and deliver smaller quantities of nutrients to the soil.

Since herbs require much less nutrition and can thrive on relatively little water, it is only natural to select organic fertilizers for their growth.

Choose a well-drained potting mix with high nitrogen and potash content for indoor plants, to promote overall growth.

The NPK ratio (nitrogen, phosphorus, and potassium ratio) indicates the ratio in which these elements are present in fertilizers. A good ratio is 4-1-1 or 5-1-1. Use a fraction of the recommended dose of fertilizers; plants often die of overfeeding rather than undernutrition.

- Fertilizers with an NPK ratio of 4-3-3 such as Jobe's Organics Herb Fertilizer protects the roots. It contains adequate phosphorus for promoting new growth.
- ALL BIO Organic Plant Food with an NPK ratio of 2-1-1 is also safe for the plants. It has growth-promoting proteins, such as Arginine, Valine, Isoleucine, and Proline. Using this enhances the flavor and taste of your herbs.
- Pepper and herb fertilizers with an NPK ratio of 11-11-40 are good for hydroponics.
- Miracle Grow Nature's Care Organic and Natural Herb Plant Food have calcium, an essential element for strong roots, besides other micronutrients.
- For 100 percent biodegradable items, choose Meghan's Garden All-Purpose Plant Food Fertilizer.
- Down to Earth Organic Garden Vegetable Fertilizer with an NPK ratio of 4-4-4 is suitable for all seasons.
- Dr. Earth® Home Grown® Tomato, Vegetable & Herb Liquid Fertilizer is suitable for topical applications or use as a compost tea. It is eco-friendly and does not harm children or pets.
- Miracle-Gro's liquid plant food is quickly absorbed by the soil and is a good option for container-grown plants.

A slow-release organic fertilizer, given once or twice a year or a doubly-diluted solution of organic liquid fertilizers with seaweeds, fish emulsion, or compost tea given sparingly once a month are all that is needed for herbs.

Feed them during their growing seasons; plants do not need food during their winter dormancy.

Add the first fertilizer one month into the growing period. Add a quarter of the recommended dose after trimming the plants. If you are using granular fertilizers, make sure the soil is moist. Water the plants after using fertilizers, allowing excess water to drain away.

Top-dress the soil lightly with compost.

Grow Herbs Naturally

Soil, water, air, and sunlight are the four crucial elements that make all the difference in growing naturally robust and vigorous plants.

Healthy Soil

Purchasing organic soil or enriching your garden soil with homemade or store-bought good-quality compost is essential.

Crop Rotation

Repeatedly growing the same crops depletes soil nutrients and makes the plants susceptible to diseases. For garden plants, crop rotation yields better results. For containers, repot every three to four years.

Black-eyed peas are good "soil-builders," they fix nitrogen into overused, tired soil.

Needs

Herbs have different needs for climate, water, sunlight, and soil conditions. Cilantro grows well in hot, humid climates, but these are unsuitable for rosemary.

Choosing which herbs to grow on your homestead is a crucial step forward, especially in the beginning. You can go more experimental once you learn more about the ways of your plants.

Thinning Out

Spacing the plants allows each one of them to achieve their potential growth. It improves airflow and checks the excess humidity that causes roots to rot. It also contains the spread of various infestations from one to the other.

Raise Garden Beds

Raising the garden bed, for outdoor plants, helps maintain the quality of soil, ensure proper drainage, and prevent the spread of infections.

Potting herbs in containers yield all of these benefits; additionally, you can shift the containers around according to the sunlight and weather conditions.

Companion planting

Companion planting aids in the mutual growth of all the plants together. Basil, garlic, thyme, lavender, and rosemary are natural choices as insect repellents. Plant nasturtiums alongside cucumber and beans to attract honey bees and butterflies.

Use Organic Fertilizers

Make your fertilizer with browns and greens from the yard and kitchen waste.

Water

During sowing, use wet but well-drained soil. Keep the soil moist to help sprouting—afterward, water when the soil feels dry to touch. Allow excess water to drain.

Trimming

Trimming your herbs and snipping off the flower heads promotes growth and prolongs the harvesting season. Keep a third of the plant intact while trimming.

Pruning

Pruning ensures the health and growth of your herbs.

6

HERBAL RECIPES FOR ANTIBIOTICS AND ANTIVIRALS

As a young girl, I used to crush marigold leaves on the superficial cuts I got by playing with my friends in the garden. I did not bother my parents, for the wounds healed naturally and painlessly, without leaving any trace. When my brother and I had flu and coughed incessantly, my mother helped us to assuage our pain with a concoction she brewed from licorice, ginger, and the leaves of the Vasaka plant (Malabar Nut). For stomach pain, she prescribed dill and ajwain (caraway) extracts, and she lovingly tended to our sprains, burns, and nicks with turmeric pastes wrapped in plantain leaves. The wounds all healed.

HEAL WOUNDS NATURALLY

In our childhood, we never needed to visit doctors, for our mother knew how to rely on nature to help us to heal. The herb garden my mother grew in our backyard had everything she needed to care for her family.

Fifteen Herbal Antibiotic Recipes

Cough Syrups

- Turmeric: Grind fresh turmeric. Add a teaspoonful to a glass of warm milk. Drink twice daily to prevent flu and to cure the cough and cold due to flu. You may use turmeric powder.
- Ginger: Did you get drenched in the rain? Grind ginger, then add a teaspoonful to a cup of hot tea. Alternatively, just throw a piece of peeled and washed ginger into the kettle, and bring it to a boil with some tea leaves. Brew for a minute before drinking. Your sore throat will vanish in no time.
- Clove: Do you have a stuffy nose and difficulty breathing due to a sudden cold? Add a drop or two of clove oil to water boiling in an uncovered pot. Inhale the warm, moist air redolent with the fragrance of clove—amazingly, you will be able to smell it again.
- Garlic: Two cloves of garlic on an empty stomach in the morning can protect you from cold.

- Black pepper: The quintessential element to relieve cough, black pepper is a must for any Indian home. It is used to make *kadha*, naturally rich in Vitamin C and flavonoids. To make kadha, dry roast ginger, cloves, black pepper, and a few basil leaves for thirty seconds. Add water; boil for five to seven minutes and strain the mixture. Store it in bottles. It is a better remedy than any other orthodox cough suppressant.
- Basil leaves: Even chewing basil leaves is said to alleviate the symptoms of flu and cold. Wash the leaves thoroughly and infuse them in hot water for ten minutes to make tea.

Toothache and Skin Infections

- Garlic: Make a paste of a clove of fresh garlic and apply it to the infected tooth a few times a day. For sharp pain, peel a clove of garlic, and bite down on it with the infected tooth. It will not only relieve the pain but will also prevent the growth of bacteria.
- Fenugreek: Do you have fenugreek seeds at home? Fenugreek has powerful astringent properties. Make tea and dip a ball of cotton wool in it. Soak the affected tooth with a moist ball to relieve pain.
- Clove oil: This is a wonderful balm for toothaches. Make your clove oil at home—crush ½ teaspoon of cloves with 1 tablespoon of olive oil. Soak the

mixture in ½ cup olive oil; allow it to rest for a week before straining out the liquid. Store in a pre-sterilized dark glass bottle to keep for about four months. To use the oil, dip a cotton bud in the oil and press it on the affected gum or tooth. Do not use it on very young children.

- Aloe vera gel: Aloe vera has strong antibiotic properties and can be used for burns, minor cuts, stings, and tooth or gum aches. Cut the edges of a leaf, including the spiny sides with a sharp knife to expose the gel. Cut the leaf into small squares. With your knife slit away the bottom side of the leaf. Scrape out the gel and use it. Alternatively, slice away both leaf surfaces, extract the gel, and blend the gel in a food processor. Pour it into a container. The refrigerated gel can be used for about ten days.

- Thyme: Thyme's antibacterial properties are an ingredient for mouthwash. Make thyme oil at home by following a simple recipe. Pluck a fistful of fresh thyme, wash and pat it dry. Crush the sprigs with a mortar and pestle to release the essential oils. Add a cup of olive or coconut oil, and heat the mixture over medium flame until it bubbles. Cool and store the mixture in sterilized glass bottles. Add two drops of thyme oil to a glass of water and gargle.

- Oregano oil: Oregano oil has two compounds, carvacrol, and thymol, with strong antibacterial and antiviral properties. It kills the harmful staphylococcus bacteria on the skin that causes furuncles, boils, and abscesses. Prepare oregano oil at home with olive oil and oregano leaves.

- Turmeric paste: Take fresh turmeric, wash and pat it dry. Slice the turmeric, and grind in a clean food processor bowl or with mortar and pestle. Rub turmeric on the skin mixed with coconut oil or mustard oil. It improves skin complexion and removes acne blemishes.
- Lavender oil: Lavender, with its strong antibacterial properties, promotes wound healing and checks common skin bacteria from infecting the wounds. Fill up a glass bottle adequately with dried lavender sprigs. Pour coconut oil in so that it covers the sprigs entirely. Secure the lid, and let the flowers fuse into oil for one week. Shake the jar occasionally. Strain the mixture to get homemade lavender oil.
- Calendula oil: Take a clean glass jar and fill it up with calendula flower petals (marigold). Fill with coconut, jojoba, sunflower, or argan oil until all the flowers are well immersed in oil. Close the lid properly and keep the bottle in a warm sunny area for a month to form the oil. Strain and store the essential oil. Calendula works well in skin infections, superficial cuts, and burns.

Herb-based Antiviral Recipes

- Oregano oil: Add 1 cup of crushed oregano herbs into 1 cup of olive oil. You can either keep the bottle in a sunny area for two weeks to make oregano oil, or place the jar in a boiler with boiling water. As the water boils, the oil in the jar is heated to make a strong infusion. Apply this to the skin for antiviral properties.
- Sage: Sage oil has strong antiviral properties against human immunodeficiency virus type 1 (HIV-1) and herpesvirus virus type 1. Soak sage leaves in carrier oils, such as coconut or olive oil. Let the mixture rest for two weeks before using it.
- Basil: Sweet basil has antiviral properties against hepatitis B, herpesvirus 1, and enterovirus 11. All are known pathogens that can cause harmful infections. Use basil tea to treat the common cold, a viral infection.
- Fennel seeds: Fennel fights the herpes virus, which causes skin infections. Fennel seeds can be eaten whole after meals to boost immunity. Make fennel tea by infusing the seeds in boiling water. To make fennel oil, boil the fennel seeds in oil, over low to medium heat, stirring occasionally, until it is a nice brown color form. It is great for your skin. Whether you have a puffy complexion or under-eye bags,

fennel oil can help to soothe and calm your skin so it
looks healthier.

- Garlic: Garlic, is a superfood that works against
  influenza A and B, HIV, HSV-1, and the common cold
  virus. Eat two cloves of garlic on an empty stomach in
  the morning. Make garlic oil by infusing it with regular
  vegetable oil. You can use this oil for cooking or for a
  massage. Fry two cloves of garlic and have them with
  mashed potatoes and a little olive oil. It tastes heavenly.
- Ginger: Ginger fights RSV, avian influenza, and
  others. Have ginger tea. Grind ginger and use the
  paste as a marinade for meat, eggs, and fish dishes.
- Oregano: Dried and crushed oregano leaves are used
  as condiments for dishes based on tomatoes and
  eggs. Use them in salads and soups to boost
  immunity.
- Lemon balm: Lemon balm extract works against
  avian influenza, herpes virus, HIV-1, and
  enterovirus. An interesting way to make lemon balm
  tincture is to infuse the leaves in vodka.
  Alternatively, use glycerine, particularly if you want
  to apply use it for children.
- Peppermint: Infuse peppermint leaves in hot water
  to brew tea with excellent antiviral properties
  against respiratory viruses.
- Rosemary: Rosemary tea has powerful antioxidant
  properties and can prevent viral infections. Brew

two sprigs of rosemary in a pot of hot water for five minutes to get a strong cup of tea. Add honey and lemon juice for taste.

- Sambucus: It is possible that the druids prepared elixirs from elderberries, which have immune boosting and antiviral properties. Add four cups of fresh elderberries or two cups of dry ones to two cups of water. Bring the water to a gentle boil, then lower the heat to a simmer. Cook for twenty minutes, pressing the berries with the back of the ladle to mash them well. Sieve the contents, pressing the berries well to extract their juices. Store the content in glass bottles for use. A slice of lemon, ginger and some honey will amplify the taste. To thicken the syrup, simmer it on the stove for a while.

- Echinacea: Echinacea was known to native Americans for its medicinal value and they used almost all parts of the plant to prepare many herbal remedies. Echinacea has antiviral and immunity-boosting properties. Wash the plant's flowers, leaves, and roots well and infuse them in a pot of steaming water. Rest it for ten minutes to make a strong tea.

- Licorice: Mix 1½ tablespoon of licorice powder with a small quantity of warm water. Add about seven ounces of sugar syrup. Use maple syrup or jaggery instead of sugar. Bring to a boil, and then lower the heat to a simmer and let it bubble, reducing the quantity to half. Strain the liquid and store it in a sterile glass bottle. Add some ginger and a small stick of cinnamon for flavor. Use licorice syrup in ice creams and sorbets, or have it along with your tea.

- Dandelion: Dandelion may be effective against dengue, a serious viral infection borne by mosquitoes. All parts of this potent antiviral herb can be eaten or infused in vinegar, oils, wines, or in water to make tea. Make jams with dandelion flowers, fruit pectin, lemon, and sugar. Bake using the flowers.
- Clove: Infuse clove in warm water and gargle with the solution. Dried cloves can be used as condiments.

NOTE: *Use all herbal oils sparingly, mixed with carrier oils.*

Make Herbal Soups

Making delicious soups with fresh garden herbs is simple, direct, and the most rewarding. The whole experience from beginning to end is a loving engagement—a connection that you transfer to your family through your cooking.

Choosing the Herbs

Parsley, especially the flat-leafed one, makes delicious soups. Add lovage to make the soup extra nourishing and flavorful.

Chives, with their subtle onion-like flavor, are a great garnish for soups and salads. Garlic, cloves, cilantro, basil, sage, thyme, and marjoram can all be included to make your delicious soups a powerhouse of flavor and nutrition.

Tomato and Basil Soup

(Kapoor, 2010)

Ingredients

- 2 onions, diced
- A few black peppercorns
- 1 bay leaf
- 8 cloves of garlic
- 2 stalks of celery, finely chopped
- 3 tablespoons of water
- 2 carrots, diced
- 20-24 tomatoes, washed and diced
- Basil leaves
- Salt and sugar to taste.
- 2 ½ cups of water

Method

- Roast onions and peppercorns lightly
- Add bay leaf
- Add garlic, celery, and 3 tablespoons of water. Stir.
- Add carrots and tomatoes.
- Add the basil leaves.
- Stir, and cook on medium flame.
- Add salt and sugar to adjust the flavor.
- Add 2 ½ cups water, bring to a boil, cover, and cook until the vegetables are cooked thoroughly.

- Strain the soup.
- You may thicken it with corn flour. Garnish with sprigs of basil and fresh cream.
- Serve.

Herbal Cocktails

Herbs Suitable for White Wines

Basil: Chardonnay, Sauvignon Blanc, Chablis

Clove: Chardonnay

Mint: Moscato, Riesling

Parsley: Sauvignon Blanc

Herbs for Red Wines

Basil: Cabernet Sauvignon, Chianti, Merlot

Clove: Pinot Noir

Rosemary: Cabernet Sauvignon, Pinot Noir

Tarragon: Merlot, Pinot Noir

Other examples are thyme, oregano, dill, chives, and laurel bay leaves for wines, and cilantro with vodka or mint with whiskey.

Garnish mocktails, such as raspberry and lime juice, with sage.

Mint Julep Recipe

Ingredients

- Mint leaves
- ¼ ounce of syrup
- 2 ounces bourbon
- Ice, crushed
- Mint leaves, for garnishing
- Angostura bitters

Method

- Mix the mint leaves with the syrup in a rocks glass or a julep cup.
- Pour in the bourbon, and pack the glass tightly with crushed ice.
- Stir until the cup is frosted on the outside.
- Garnish with mint sprigs and a few drops of Angostura bitters.

Herbal Concentrate

Herbal concentrates ensure a year-round supply of your most precious herbs. They are surprisingly easy to make with only two ingredients, herbs, and good quality vegetable oil, preferably extra virgin olive oil.

Most herbs, such as basil, cilantro, sage, mint, rosemary, and lemon verbena, can be turned into concentrates. Store them like pesto or butter, frozen in the freezer compartment of your refrigerator. Since they are steeped in oil, they do not lose their freshness over time, nor do they become hard and crystallized.

Basil Concentrate

Take basil leaves and wash them well. You can use dry basil leaves as an alternative. Throw them in a food processor bowl. As you pulse, drizzle olive oil slowly in, to get a smooth blend. Continue pouring the oil until the herbs are steeped in it. Scrape the bowl and collect your concentrate in small containers. Label them for future use.

Herbal Expectorants

Make cough syrups with holy basil, licorice, and ginger. A teaspoonful of this mixture, three times a day works as the best expectorant and reduces respiratory inflammation.

Vasaka leaves, ginger, and basil leaves have always been used as expectorants in India.

Vasaka Basil Decoction

- Collect healthy Vasaka and basil leaves.
- Wash the leaves well.
- Grind the leaves, adding a little bit of water.
- Add licorice, ginger, and cinnamon in small quantities and mix everything well.

- In a pot boil the leaves with one quart of water until the solution becomes one-third of the original volume.
- Strain the solution, cool it, and pour it into a glass bottle.

Herbal Poultices

Many herbs reduce the pain and swelling of sprained joints, the inflammation of burnt tissues, and the irritation caused by insect bites and stings. Herbal pastes are applied directly to the affected areas. To ensure longer contact, bandage the affected part with a thin gauze or clean linen. Alternatively, the poultice can be placed inside a clean sock or in a cloth bag.

An herbal poultice can be hot to induce sweating and improve blood flow, or cold to relieve pain and sunburn.

Turmeric Paste

Of all the herbs, turmeric is best known for its medicinal and pain-relieving abilities. To make turmeric paste, take a few pieces of fresh turmeric, wash off the dirt, and grind them in a blender. Alternatively, turmeric powder or dry turmeric can be used.

Grind the turmeric with oil, such as mustard or coconut oil, which is known for its anti-infective properties. Apply the poultice to the affected area and bandage it. Turmeric reduces joint pain, sunburn, and many other external inflammations.

Herbal Tincture

The fundamental difference between tinctures and extracts is the solvent used. For tinctures, it is alcohol. Extracts may use glycerine, water, or vinegar as solvents. However, vodka is the preferred medium because of its ability to bring out the flavor of the herbs.

But why tinctures? *They are concentrated, stable, readily available, and easily administered forms of herbs.* We can use tinctures as diet supplements for wellness therapy and medicinal purposes.

The effects of tinctures depend on their content, concentration, dosages, and the reason for which they are prescribed. As with herbs, they work wonders for some and not so well for a few others. They must be prescribed by an herbalist.

Tinctures are economical and effective, are readily available, and most people depend on them for at least some part of their treatment.

Tinctures of fresh leaves and flowers

- Fill a jar to two-thirds of its volume with the cleaned and ground ingredients.
- Pour in vodka until the bottle is full. The herbs should move inside when the jar is shaken.

- Cover the jar.

Tinctures of dried leaves, flowers, and berries

Fill half of the jar using dry ingredients and pour vodka from the top.

For dry roots, berries, and stems fill only one-third of the jar because dry items eventually swell up in alcohol.

Use 40-50 percent weight by volume for most herbs.

For aromatic roots, herbs, and those with higher moisture content, use 67.5-70 percent alcohol (Raychel, 2017).

Herbal First-Aid

Our first-aid boxes are for emergencies when there is no pharmacy or doctor available near an accident. From beestings and insect bites to cuts and abrasions, first-aid boxes are often the saviors of many incidents and can avoid visits to a hospital's emergency room.

Lavender oil

Lavender oil is good for wounds. However, some may be allergic to it.

Calendula

Calendula works like magic when applied to superficial burns, rashes, insect bites, and stings, and moisturizes dry skin.

Aloe Vera gel or cattail gel

Both varieties of herbs grow worldwide, and their gels soothe burns, moisturize skin, and are good for sunburn.

Common Yarrow

Common Yarrow is native to North America. Its leaves, like marigolds, soothe and heal when crushed and applied to wounds and burns. Yarrow belongs to the genus Achillea, derived from Achilles, and extracts of the leaves were used to treat soldiers' wounds. A tea of common yarrow leaves treats headaches and colds.

Arnica

Arnica is widely cultivated in North America. This medicinal herb can be applied to the skin as creams, ointments, and tinctures. It relieves headaches and reduces pain and inflammation.

7

DIY YOUR HERBAL HOUSEHOLD PRODUCTS

Many believe the widespread use of chemicals in daily life started in the eighteenth century. Mankind's rampant use of chemicals is destroying our natural environment. In the bygone days, agriculturists were more tuned to nature, and they used wildflowers and plants, such as lupin and cucumber to ward off pests. Herbal products are more sustainable and eco-friendlier, and using them is safer for all of us.

NATURE'S CARE

Women used henna to dye their hair; indigo, marigold, sunflowers, cosmos, and dahlias to color their clothes; and extracts from lavender, sandalwood, and rose to make cleansers for their faces. Neem extract was the usual disinfectant for our household, and it worked. We used *reetha* (Indian soapberry) to shampoo our hair. It did not deplete our tresses of their natural oils, keeping them shiny and silky.

In this chapter, we will create history with our petite DIY crafts. Let us begin!

Homemade Exfoliating Soap

To make good quality exfoliating soaps, we will need 6 ounces of organic melt and pour soap and one tablespoon of coconut oil as a base. Melt and pour soaps are pre-made soap bases with fatty acids, glycerine, and other natural elements. Into this, we will mix in the essential oils and other exfoliating agents to get three different soap varieties.

Below are three different fragrances, each with a different exfoliating agent. Choose the one that best suits your skin, and the aromas you love. The basic method of preparation is given separately below.

Rosemary-Lemon Soap with Cornmeal

Cornmeal is a good exfoliating agent for any sensitive skin. The essential oils of the herbs are not only fragrant but also anti-infective.

Ingredients

- 10 drops each of lemon and rosemary essential oils.
- 1 tablespoon of cornmeal

Coffee-Cinnamon-Ginger-Orange Soap

Ingredients

- 15 drops of cinnamon bark essential oil
- 10 drops of ginger essential oil
- 10 drops of orange essential oil
- 2 tablespoons of coffee grounds (scrubbing agent)

Geranium-Patchouli with Himalayan Pink Salt

This soap has pink salt as the scrubbing agent and the scent of geraniums.

Ingredients

- 10 drops of patchouli essential oil
- 5 drops of geranium oil
- 1-2 tablespoons of Himalayan pink salt

Method

- Cut the readymade soap into 1" cubes.
- Melt the soap pieces and coconut oil together.
- Stir the mixture occasionally to prevent clumping.
- Add the essential oils to the melted mixture and stir to mix well.
- Pour the exfoliating agent slowly, stirring continuously to mix the ingredients before they solidify. Pour into the soap mold.

You can also use other essential oils, such as lavender and thyme. The soaps make wonderful gifts!

DIY Herbal Body Lotions

Make your own body lotion at home, and it will be far better and safer than the store-bought chemical-packed ones (Maslowski, 2014).

Ingredients

- 1 cup of oil. Any vegetable oil, such as olive, coconut, grapefruit, hempseed, or safflower will do. Infused oils, such as calendula or lavender are excellent choices. For naturally occurring Vitamin E oils, choose macadamia and hazelnut oils.
- Wax, its amount, when mixed with the oil, should make 1¼ cup.
- Shea or cocoa butter, optional
- ½ cup of water
- ⅛ teaspoon of borax
- A few drops of the pure essential oils of your choice

Method

- Melt oil and wax in a large bowl, in a microwave. Add any butter, such as shea or cocoa butter at this stage.
- In a pot, bring the water to a boil. Add the borax and stir. Keep it hot. Now, pour the oil mixture into the water-borax solution slowly, as it may boil and rise to the surface. At all stages, the liquid must be very hot; otherwise, it will not cream.
- Blending the mixture in a blender or with a whisk, for a few minutes, will help it to cream.
- Mix in the essential oil and your body lotion is ready for use.

This DIY cream can evolve into any other by simply tweaking the ingredients. For instance, lavender oil and aloe water make a suntan lotion, ginger and turmeric make a cream for joint symptoms, rosemary for foot cream, and calendula for skin irritation and minor burns.

DIY Body Lotion

(Wills, 2022)

Ingredients

- 73 g of distilled water
- 2 g glycerine
- 5 g shea butter

- 14 g sunflower oil
- 6 g emulsifying wax NF
- 16 drops of essential oils of your choice

Method

Water Component

- Boil water, add glycerine and pour it into a heatproof jug.

Oil Component

- Mix all the oily components, such as the shea butter, sunflower oil, and wax together in the same jug.
- Heat some water in a double boiler pot with the bottom pot that acts as a water bath. This is done to give precise temperature control. Put the oil component into the pot first and then add the water component slowly, taking care the mixture does not overflow.
- The oils melt and form an emulsion. It can take about half an hour. Let it sit in the hot water bath for some time to ensure thorough mixing.
- Remove from the water bath and give it a good stir to make a thick lotion. This may take about ten minutes.
- Add the essential oils and a few drops of a preservative if required.

- Pour into a pump bottle.

DIY Salves

Salves are easy to make at home. The herbs that make good salves are turmeric, comfrey, ginger, lavender, calendula, arnica, thyme, yarrow, and echinacea roots.

Ingredients

- Beeswax: 1 ounce. For softer salves use less of it and more for firmer ones.
- Herbal oil: 4 ounces

Method

- Melt the beeswax in a small bowl.
- Add herbal oils of choice.
- Stir over low heat until properly mixed.
- Pour the mixture while still warm into a glass jar.
- Store in a cool dry place for use.

DIY Mouthwash

Various herbs, such as clove, peppermint, and rosemary, are used in making mouthwash.

Ingredients

- 1 teaspoon of whole cloves

- 2 tablespoons of dried peppermint leaves
- 1 tablespoon of dried rosemary
- 20 drops of essential oils, such as cinnamon or peppermint.
- 8 ounces of 80 percent ethyl alcohol (rum/vodka)

Method

- Make a tincture with these ingredients. The herbs must sit in the alcohol for a fortnight before straining the liquid with a clean cheesecloth into a bottle fitted with a tight lid.
- Store in a cool dry place.

DIY Insect Repellants

With Essential Oils

- ½ teaspoon catnip oil
- 1 cup of water
- 1 cup isopropyl alcohol

Method

- Mix these ingredients and store them in a pump bottle.

Alternatively, use:

- ½ teaspoon of citronella or lemongrass oil
- 2 cups of witch hazel
- 1 tablespoon of apple cider vinegar

Mix well and store in a pump bottle.

With Whole Herbs

Make a spray with:

- Fresh mint
- Basil
- Lavender leaves

Steep for about five minutes in a cup of boiling water and strain. Add a cup of witch hazel as an alcohol base.

Make a spray with:

- 4 tablespoons of dried cloves
- catnip
- lavender
- peppermint

Boil the leaves in a cup of water. Strain to use.

DIY Cleaners

Make herbal cleaners and use them fearlessly in your home without having to worry about the children or your pets, and enjoy the fresh aroma of the essential oils as a bonus.

Ingredients

- 8 ounces distilled white vinegar
- 6 ounces distilled water
- 2 ounces vodka
- 10 drops of lavender oil
- 5 drops of rosemary oil
- 5 drops of lemon oil

Mix all the components and pour them into a large spray bottle. Shake well before using.

DIY Sanitizer

We all have to use hand sanitizer, more so in the aftermath of the pandemic. Make your own sanitizer and carry a small bottle with you.

Ingredients

- Neem leaves
- Basil leaves
- Water: 1 quart
- Aloe vera
- Alum: 10 g

- Camphor: 10 g

Method

- Boil the fresh or dried leaves of the herbs in water. Add aloe gel and boil some more. Add alum and camphor and allow the mixture to cool.
- Camphor is antiviral and antibacterial besides having a cooling effect. Alum has antibacterial and antifungal properties.

DIY Aromatizers

Give your office and home the beautiful fragrance and freshness of herbs by preparing simple yet useful aromatizers.

Ingredients

- Your favorite essential oil
- 3 ounces of ethyl alcohol
- 12 ounces of distilled water solution with calendula, catnip, chamomile, or sage

Combine all of the ingredients and store the mixture in a spray bottle. Shake well before using on furniture or furnishings.

Aromatic Bags

Stuff some dried aromatic herbs and flowers in a small pouch or tote bag. Add a few drops of essential oil of your choice to this collection. Tie the neck of the pouch. Use this aromatic pouch in the corners of your bedroom.

8

MAKING MONEY FROM HERBAL HOMESTEADING

Herbal Homesteading is a resource that supplies us with nutritious choices, and natural household products for everyday use. Why not turn this into a profitable venture?

STEPPING OUT

Once we become familiar with growing herbs, we may consider other options that can make us successful as herbalists. There is a demand for organic herbal products in the market, and it is increasing. More people are now aware of the beneficial nature of herbal products in their homes and their surroundings. They choose them over synthetic ones.

What would be the most profitable herbs to grow? How can we start our venture as an herbalist? These are some questions that this chapter will now examine.

Most Profitable Herbs

When thinking about business ventures we must know which herbs are in demand.

Basil

Basil is the most popular herb for culinary and medicinal uses. It grows well in containers and outdoors, and is not a fussy grower. Basil needs warmer weather conditions. Keep it indoors on the windowsill in winter where it can get sunlight.

Chives

Chives are common ingredients for various types of cooking. It grows in cooler regions.

Cilantro

Vegetable markets are always asking for fresh cilantro. Growing it is profitable.

Oregano

Oregano has a special appeal in cooking Italian food. Grow this popular herb to add value to your urban homestead.

Chamomile

Chamomile tea is known for its calming effects. Grow chamomile to produce organic tea, home products, and natural insecticides.

Catnip

Catnip is easy to grow. It has medicinal value and pet lovers are always on the lookout for toys stuffed with catnip.

Lavender

Lavender fills up your homestead with its color and fragrance. Its medicinal value earns lavender a guaranteed position in a homestead.

Grow These Rare Herbs

Herbs, such as basil and chives are commonly grown in most homes. These much sought-after herbs will help give your homestead an edge.

Anise

The lavender flowers of anise and their slender stalks have medicinal value and are used in many sweet and savory dishes.

Brahmi

These innocuous herbs are well known in Ayurveda for improving concentration and relieving stress and anxiety. They grow happily on the windowsill.

Holy Basil

This plant with its green and purple leaves and purple flowers is a powerhouse of medicinal properties. Grow it to make herbal teas and other medicines.

Marshmallow

Everyone loves marshmallows. It grows easily and has medicinal properties.

Sorrel

Sorrel is good for kidney function, heart health, eyesight, and immune function. It may have anticancer effects. Sorrel develops a lemon flavor in winter and is used in making soups, salads, and sauces.

Selling Herbs and Seeds

Selling your homegrown produce is the best way for a startup. Fresh herbs, such as cilantro, chives, rosemary, and thyme are always in demand.

Many customers love dried herbs to make tea, beverages, and concoctions that are good for cold and flu.

You can make smoking mixtures to repel mosquitoes and flies or even small test samples to showcase your products.

Start Your Business

Plan which herbs to grow and analyze why. The first thing to consider would be the cost of starting a venture. The next step is identifying the target population and fixing the value of the products.

The question that automatically arises is where to set up a startup. Going into costly propositions may not be practical at the outset. Deciding to book a spot at the local farmers' market, or a home-based approach only seems more appropriate.

To make your venture more profitable, organize a tea party where your friends, family, and neighbors can learn about the products they can purchase from you. Offer them small gifts, such as herbal soap, or an air freshener This way it will be possible to determine which products are more in demand and, generally, what are people looking for.

Any venture is an educational journey with a certain desti- nation. As one progresses, evaluation of every step and assessing their feasibility and profitability are the keys to a successful venture.

Do not forget to name your business. In the future, it may turn into a million-dollar corporation!

Become A Teacher

The beauty of growing herbs lies in their richness of poten- tial. What often starts out as a hobby may soon evolve into a passion. A passion may turn into a vocation. All this happens naturally, and many herbalists have grown into the profession.

Being an herbalist does not mean that one is consecrated to a single job opportunity. Contrarily, there are many options. Teaching about herbs is just one of those.

Take community classes, organize workshops, online classes, podcasts, and master classes. Teach others about the benefits of herbs, how to grow them and how to make natural products out of them. Teaching others to cook, make beverages, and bake with many herbs is a wonderful vocation.

As a professional, one may contribute to scientific research, and write in journals, publications, magazines, and blogs. Having a website for a business can help it to proliferate.

One may start a consultancy, offering medicinal and nutritional counseling to others. Sharing your knowledge about herbs with others helps you to connect with them in matters relating to personal health and hygiene. In time, you might start an apothecary to prescribe your medicines to people in need.

A SHORT MESSAGE FROM THE AUTHOR

Hey, are you enjoying the book? I'd love to hear your thoughts!

Many readers do not know how hard reviews are to come by, and how much they help an author.

Customer Reviews

⭐⭐⭐⭐⭐ 2
5.0 out of 5 stars ▾

5 star	▮▮▮▮▮	100%
4 star		0%
3 star		0%
2 star		0%
1 star		0%

Share your thoughts with other customers

Write a customer review ⬅

See all verified purchase reviews ›

I would be incredibly grateful if you could take just 60 seconds to write a brief review on Amazon, even if it's just a few sentences!

>> Click here to leave a quick review [PUT YOUR REVIEW LINK HERE]

Thank you for taking the time to share your thoughts!

Your review will genuinely make a difference for me and help gain exposure for my work.

Pushpa Puar

CONCLUSION

The alarming ways in which the world relies on allopathic medicines have concerned me time and again. One issue that I have with conventional forms of medication is that they hardly ever seem to look at the internal or overarching conditions that lead to a particular health concern. Notwithstanding, all modern medicine has its roots in the traditional forms of healing which derived ways to heal ailments from nature.

I started my garden patch by growing flowers, but I was soon conquered by the beauty and simplicity of herbs. Gradually I entered their realm and they engulfed my senses with their richness of aroma and texture. I learned their healing properties; sometimes the knowledge was passed down from my elders, and sometimes I learned by serendipity. What I did learn encouraged me to delve further into the realm of naturotherapy. Here is a science where you do the healing for yourself, and nature chimes in to help show the way.

I discovered that herbal homesteading does not need many resources, and therein lies its beauty. I have not looked back. My herbs have nurtured my family, neighborhood, and my community with the silent benevolence that comes so naturally with them.

If we are talking about inclusivity, then lives without herbs remain incomplete.

REFERENCES

Hassani, N. (2021, August 19). Do Herbs Need to Be Fertilized? Know When and How Much to Fertilize. *the spruce*. Https://Www.Thespruce.Com/Best-Fertilizers-for-Awesome-Herbs-1761848.

How to Make Herbal Tinctures. (2022). *Mountain Rose Herbs*. Https://Blog.Mountainroseherbs.Com/Guide-Tinctures-Extracts.

How To Plan And Plant A Medicinal Garden. (2019, September 14). *The Homestead Lady*. Https://Homesteadlady.Com/How-to-Plan-and-Plant-a-Medicinal-Herb-Garden/.

Kapoor, S. (2010). *Tasty Eating for Healthy Living*. Popular Prakashan Pvt Ld.

Maslowski, D. (2022). How to Make an Herbal Body Cream. *DIY Natural*. Https://Www.Diynatural.Com/Herbal-Homemade-Body-Lotion/.

Shoba, G., Joy, D., Joseph, T., Majeed, M., Rajendran, R., & Srinivas, P. (1998). Influence of Piperine on the Pharmacokinetics of Curcumin in Animals and Human Volunteers. *Planta Medica*, 64(04), 353–356. https://doi.org/10.1055/s-2006-957450.

Wills, A. (2022). How To Make Homemade Body Lotion From Scratch. *Savvy Homemade*. Https://Www.Savvyhomemade.Com/Homemade-Body-Lotion-Recipes/.

Made in the USA
Monee, IL
28 December 2023

50662129R00100